Roll Up Your Sleeves and Get to Work:
The *Bald Truth* About Making Things Happen

by Rick Kolster, CBC

Copyright © 2014
Published in the United States by

Insight Publishing Company
707 W. Main Street Suite 5
Sevierville, Tennessee 37862
www.insightpublishing.com
Cover by Steve Wilson
Formatting and Layout by Chris Ott

Disclaimer: This book is a compilation of ideas from numerous experts who have each contributed a chapter. As such, the views expressed in each chapter are of those who were interviewed and not necessarily of the interviewer or Insight Publishing.

ISBN- 978-1-60013-140-0

What People Are Saying About *Roll Up Your Sleeves and Get to Work!*

" With Roll Up Your Sleeves . . . Coach Rick Kolster unites both business and life coaching in a totally practical, imaginative, and useful way. I found myself thinking in new ways about common obstacles we too often ignore and feeling inspired to overcome them! This book is a great tool for young and old, in business or in personal life, and especially for those who aspire to lead others. "

—Major General Bill Essex, USAF, Ret.

" Coach Rick writes *Roll Up Your Sleeves and Get to Work* just like he speaks— straightforward and to the point. His "listen, learn, and live" approach puts real change into three simple steps. A must-read that leaves the audience focused and inspired. "

—Judy Gaman, author and co-host of *The Staying Young Show*

" If life were easy and without serious challenges, there wouldn't be a need for Coach Rick Kolster. But life isn't that way, of course. I've known Coach Rick for a decade, and it's wonderful to see him finally sum up his life's work to help others in this wonderful book. "

—Dave Lieber, Watchdog columnist, *The Dallas Morning News*

" Is it time to make your life your own? In *Roll Up Your Sleeves . . .* Coach Rick asks you powerful questions and gives you practical exercises to get on point, on purpose and achieving your success in every aspect of your life now. "

—Holly Duckworth, CAE, CMP, Chief Connections Officer

To Mom and Dad: I love and miss you.

To all those who have helped and shared their inspiration with me and shaped me into the man I am today.

To my two beautiful daughters, Megan and Lauren: I am blessed and humbled to have two of the greatest kids ever. I'm proud of the wonderful, God-fearing and loving young women you have become.

Finally, to all the coaches I have had the privilege to be mentored by and learn from. You are doing great work. Keep it up . . . and, as I was told early on, "Do good things. Don't be the one to screw it up for the rest of us!"

CONTENTS

Foreword by Pat Cline 1

Prologue: Living with Rich and Sally 3

How to Use This Book 5

Part 1: Listen 7

1.1 Attitude 9

1.2 Belief 15

1.3 Purpose 19

Part 2: Learn 25

2.1 Duplicate others 27

2.2 Get a mentor—Get a coach 33

2.3 Accountability and Goal-setting 41

Part 3: Live 53

3.1 Commitment and Hard Work 55

3.2 Balance 65

3.3 Sometimes it's just pure luck! 71

Epilogue: Never be Satisfied 75

About the Author 77

Coach Rick's 12 Commandments for Success 79

Coach Rick's 12 Commandments for Success 81

Balance Wheel 83

Coach Rick's GPS Worksheet 85

Beliefs Worksheet 87

Coach Rick's 12 Commandments To Go 89

When I was sixteen, I watched my father work so hard he couldn't enjoy life. A few years later, he passed away at age fifty. I'll spare you the long version but I set a goal back then to retire by age fifty. As a teenager, I didn't know much about setting goals but that one was crystal clear. Fast forward some thirty years later, I started working with Coach Rick Kolster. I had been busy building companies my entire career using many of the principles Rick teaches. I helped lead one company from a startup to a multi-billion dollar market value. Two years after I started working with Rick, I announced my retirement. I was fifty.

To tell you the truth, I wasn't very good at being retired so I pulled myself out of retirement and I am working again, but on very different terms. I'm applying the science of goal setting and achievement and I'm balancing my personal and professional life at a much better level. I am grateful for the principles that Coach Rick led me to employ in my life.

Goals and achievement are most often discussed in terms of professional aspects—the career or the money. I'm here to tell you that personal goals and personal growth are just as important. The goals Rick helped me crystallize had to do with balance; raising my children, strengthening my marriage, improving my health, and what I wanted the next stage of my life to look like. As you think about growth, goal setting, and achievement, I challenge you to think about what's truly important.

One of the very best in the coaching business is author, speaker, and coach, John C. Maxwell. He states in his book, *The 15 Invaluable Laws of Growth*, that "In order to reach your potential, you must grow and in order to grow, you must be intentional about it." What is your potential? Are you intentional about reaching it? What are your specific goals? How will you achieve them? Is your plan clear?

Most people "go with the flow" and move through life going where their days take them. They might take a few accidental minutes to dream about what they want. They might dream about who they want to be. They might hope something miraculous will happen that will allow them to break out of the status quo, but they don't know how to make it happen. Relatively few of the seven billion people on this planet roll up their sleeves and *make* it happen. Relatively few take full responsibility for themselves, for their situation, and for their growth. Those few people hold themselves accountable for their own success . . . and they succeed.

At its core, this book is about accountability. Yes, this book is filled with more than just the concepts of accountability, such as thought-provoking questions and powerful exercises to get you on track and Rick's "listen, learn, and live" concepts that

I

if applied will help you make positive life changes. Rick is a tell-it-like-it-is kind of man and this book is no different. His straightforward, no-nonsense, let's get to work approach is how this book is written. Rick is not about fluff—he is action-oriented. This book is intended to get you thinking, to challenge the habits that may be limiting you and preventing you from reaching your potential. It may be time to swap those habits for ones that serve you better.

Rick is a highly experienced coach and I hope that reading this book will be like having Rick as *your* personal coach. His goal with this book is to inspire you to go deeper, take action, and reach your potential. I believe that if you follow the guidelines and principles in this book you will be able to make your life excel on all levels.

Let's return to the concept of accountability for a moment. Whether or not this book makes a difference in your life has little to do with this book. It depends on you and whether or not you are willing to work to make yourself and your life better. If you are not willing to commit to your own growth, then stop reading now and gift or re-gift this book.

If you are willing to roll up your sleeves and get to work, then I challenge you to do so.

I was the first-born son of a working-class family in the late fifties. My dad, Rich, dug the holes for telephone poles and my mom, Sally, was a part-time seamstress and full-time mother. While I was number one, it didn't last for long. Soon two sisters came along and then eight years after I was born, my brother showed up to even the score.

Raising four kids in the sixties was tough, just as it was for a hundred years before and will be for a hundred years after. Ward and June Cleaver did *not* live at our house. Mom and Dad were good parents, but trying to deal with four kids eight years apart in age was a challenge. I found that as the oldest, I had to learn to fend for myself. I led the way, but the two girls following in my footsteps got a lot more attention from our parents. Dad was a working guy, blue collar all the way. If it had to be done, Dad just did it. He could fix anything around the house. The car's oil needed changing or the brakes needed replacing? No need to send it out to the shop or call in a repair guy. We did it ourselves. This is where I learned the value of hard work—from my parents.

Mom was the stable one in the family, the one who stayed home with the kids, worked from home when needed, and ran the house. Breakfast was ready at 7:00 AM, every day. Dinner was ready at 6:00 every night without fail. She made our lunches and sewed the clothes we wore. Mom was a seamstress by trade, so all our clothes were homemade. We really hated wearing this stuff—we weren't exactly taking the fashion world by storm. Looking back, I now know those shirts and dresses were made with real love. Ultimately once we kids were old enough to be left alone, she began a second career as a banker. I can see now how hard my parents worked to keep up with us kids.

Robert Fulghum made big bucks on a book called *All I Really Need to Know I Learned in Kindergarten.* Well, all I ever needed to know I learned from my parents. My dad would give you the shirt off his back, make you laugh with his humor (off color as it was at times), and help out in any way if you needed it. Mom was cut from the same cloth. They understood what it took to survive and provide for themselves and their family, and they didn't complain or question or hesitate—they just got on with it.

They themselves came from working families, too. "If it is to be it is up to me" could be the family motto. Dad taught me to fix cars, run electrical wires, plumbing, yard work, splitting firewood, and so many other practical skills. He also taught me to love reading.

At first glance you wouldn't take Dad for a big reader, but every payday, he would bring home paperbacks that he would read and then hand to me. They were mostly action series and military fiction, with muscle-bound, testosterone-laced heroes who could take me into another world. To this day, I love to escape into a good action or military book. Now I love to read all kinds of other stuff too, and I credit my dad for that as well. Reading is a great way to learn, and learning is such a huge part of success that there's a whole section in this book devoted to it.

The most important thing I learned from Dad was that if you tried, learned what you needed to, and took action on it, you could do anything. He worked his tail off. He had a full-time job with the telephone company, a part-time job at a gas/service station, and a third helping his friend as a laborer setting tile. When he wasn't working at a job, he was working around the house.

He wasn't a touchy-feely guy, but I loved hanging out with him and watching him work, and I knew he loved me.

Here are some of the life lessons I learned from the two best parents a kid could have.

This book is about taking action. If you want your life to be different, you have to *make* it different. That means rolling up your sleeves and taking action.

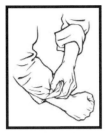

In each section of the book, there's a part called "**ROLL 'EM!**" marked with the graphic you see here. These are exercises meant to help you take action on the lessons of the book. Most of these exercises involve writing things down. Successful people know you can't hold all the important stuff in your head, and sometimes you have to take things out and look at them in a very concrete way in order to learn.

So I suggest that you get a journal, if you don't already have one, and keep it close to this book. You could use your smart phone or tablet or computer for this too; just make sure that whatever you use is easy for you to write in. Your tiny little phone keyboard is probably not going to cut it for writing a couple of paragraphs or a page, but hey—they're your thumbs. Do whatever works for you.

The main thing about this book is that it's not going to help you at all if you don't do anything with it. Books are great as far as they go, but let's face it—nobody ever learned how to swim from reading a book. If you want to learn to swim, you have to get into the water. If you want to change your life, you have to take real action in the real world, not just read about it or think about it or write about it (although those steps are important too).

Taking action is how you are going to build the life you want. **So let's roll up our sleeves and get to work!**

I had three goals in writing this book: to *inform*, to *inspire*, and to *incite* you, the reader. In turn, I hope you'll hold up your end of the bargain by listening, learning, and living—the three "Ls" that lead to personal success. Let's start with listening.

I learned what I learned from my parents by paying attention to what they said and did. Listening is how we get information, and having information is the first step toward achieving the results you want.

Listening isn't just about what you do with your ears, and hearing is not the same thing as listening. You hear all kinds of stuff all the time—good news, bad news, information, entertainment, and plain old noise. You also hear clear messages in what people around you do. You've heard the saying "actions speak louder than words," and it's true. The things people do tell you loud and clear what kind of people they are. There's plenty to hear all around you. The question is, what are you going to listen to, and what are you going to ignore?

Listening means paying attention. It means soaking up whatever value there is in what you hear, and making sure you remember the important stuff so you can do something with it later. When your best friend or your spouse says something to you, do you just say, "Yeah, sure," and move on with your life, or do you really listen to what he or she is trying to tell you? Chances are there's something worthwhile there if you choose to listen.

On the other hand, there's a lot of crap, if you'll pardon the expression, coming into your world every day, too. The news is a mess. People say things to you that are not kind or helpful. Heck, you say things to yourself, inside your own head, that no decent person would ever say out loud to another human being. What are you listening to? Do you let the negative stuff get to you? Do you let it affect how you live your life?

Your attitudes and beliefs evolve based on how you listen and what you hear. This starts at the moment you're born and continues all your life. When you decide what matters, you gain purpose and will, and that makes it more clear what's worth listening to and what's not. So in this section we're going to look at attitude, belief, and purpose. I'll do my best to inform, and I hope you'll do your best to listen. From there, it's up to you to decide where the value is.

How do you wake up every morning? What is your attitude when your feet hit the floor? Before I took a good look at the way I was thinking I used to wake up every morning and start the day with some words

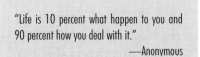

that don't really belong in a business book. What a way to start the day, right? The first word out of my mouth was one I never want my kids to use.

I used to start every day with a negative thought, an attitude of loss, not gain. This is what held me back for so long. Maybe it's holding you back, too. How many times have you seen something about positive attitude or affirmations or keeping your chin up, and just shook your head and said, "Wow, what a bunch of losers with their nursery school garbage." Well, if those guys are richer, happier, and more successful than you are, who exactly is the loser here?

Having a positive attitude isn't the same thing as pretending everything is happy and perfect. It's about knowing where you're going, being grateful for what you have, and looking for the upside in everything. We are not destined for mediocrity. We are wonderful creations made to be successful. Embrace this attitude daily and only good can come from it.

Most of the world looks at the things they cannot do rather than the things they can do. We approach life from a scarcity perspective. Scarcity mentality focuses on all the limits and everything that's missing or wrong in the world. If you have scarcity mentality, you're scrambling to get the biggest piece you can of a pie that's not big enough to feed everyone. All you see is what is holding you back and what is not possible. But remember, I said "most of the world" has this perspective. If you see things this way sometimes, or even most of the time, you're pretty typical. But how does that outlook affect your life?

Scarcity mentality is an attitude, and by the time you are an adult, it's ingrained pretty deep—to the point where you don't even realize how it is coloring your view of the world. And what's more, that attitude affects how you see other people, and can be taught to the people in your life who look up to you, such as your kids, for example.

I am positive that our parents and their parents and their parents didn't wake up in the early morning hours thinking "How can I hold my children back from greatness?" Of course not! They went about trying to raise us as best they could. And if you're a parent, you're doing the same thing. But kids don't come with an instruction manual, and having a kid doesn't magically turn your entire way of seeing the world 180 degrees. Parenting is trial-and-error, and you do the best you can with what you have. If what you have is a scarcity mentality, you could be holding your kids back without even realizing it.

Case in point: For the longest time I was told that I should be a mechanic. My dad said I was good with my hands and that I was big and strong and that was his picture of a mechanic. I even started to believe it at some point.

Now don't get me wrong, I'm not knocking mechanics. I've seen the same thing happen to kids who got pushed and pushed to go to college and be a lawyer or a doctor when what they wanted most in this world was to be a mechanic. The point is that my dad's belief about what I could and should do with my life was driven by his assumptions, and after awhile, I just accepted his belief. He's my dad—he must be right! But he wasn't thinking about what I might want to do, or what I might be capable of or interested in doing. He was just looking at what was in front of him and filtering it through his assumptions.

I had to realize what was going on there before I could make the changes necessary to take the next step in my success journey. I had to decide what I wanted, take charge of my life, and see how my own attitude was going to make or break me. Until you take a hard look at your attitude, you will be stuck where you are.

A positive attitude lets you overcome all the challenges of day-to-day life. Every day we deal with rude people, uncooperative clients, unsafe drivers on the road—a million things eat away at our patience and our moods. Yet all these things can be addressed with a positive attitude—an attitude of abundance that says there's plenty for everybody if we choose to see and accept the blessings that are right in front of us.

I believe that we choose our attitude daily. We make a choice in the attitude we will embrace. Is yours a winner or a loser? Does it come with a list of reasons why you're going to fail and everything is going to go wrong, or is it positive and powerful? Henry Ford said, "If you think you can or you think you can't, you are right." What attitude did you bring into today? What attitude will you bring to tomorrow?

A good friend of mine has one of the best attitudes I have ever seen. He has reached heights of success that most of us would never have imagined. He has been on television and in movies, is a sought-after speaker, and has his own infomercial. He wakes up every day like this: He rolls out of bed, claps his hands together, and says out loud, "It's gonna be a *great day*!" WOW—now that is the way to start things off. Tell yourself it is going to be a great day. That sure beats waking up with a cuss word, right?

The Mechanics of Attitude

Remember, in the introduction of this section, I said that one of my goals was to inform. Knowing a little bit about how attitudes work can help you understand where they come from and how you can change them using the same process that created them in the first place.

Attitudes are habits of thought, and most of them emerge very early. Ninety-five percent of all attitudes are developed before the age of five. By the time we reach adulthood, we have held most of our attitudes for so long, we don't even think of them as attitudes or notice how they influence how we see the world. The world just is what it is. It doesn't even occur to us that someone else may see it differently, or that it might *be* different from what we see. We don't see the world as it is. We see it as *we* are.

Most people tend to think more negatively than positively, most of the time, and this feeds and is fed by our life experience. Emphasis on the negative seems to attract us for some crazy reason—we go toward it like moths to a flame. Think of the adage "if it bleeds, it leads." Television, newspapers, all forms of media really work the negative, especially if it's spectacular, shocking, and bloody. If a movie has a happy ending, people will say it was "not realistic." The worst part is that all this negative stuff accumulates in our brains as "evidence" that life is hard, that we'll never be good enough, and that divorces and plane crashes are more normal than living a good life and dying of old age. Pretty soon we believe we have "proof" that life sucks, and that makes our attitudes even *more* negative.

But sniper attacks and the latest cause of cancer are *not* normal. They make headlines *because* they are not normal. If we want to have a more positive experience of life, we have to see things differently. Improvement begins with a change in our attitudes. We have to make sure the attitudes that we're carrying with us are actually taking us closer to our goals and objectives and not further away.

Attitude affects results. Once we see things differently, we see different things. When we do things differently, we do different things. Every day, every moment of every day, from the time you get up in the morning until you go to bed at night, attitude affects results.

In fact, attitude affects everything. If you are ever unsatisfied with the results you are getting with a relationship, a challenge, a project, a problem, or even just a conversation, look inside yourself first. How are you showing up to the situation and how is your attitude affecting it? Chances are, a change of your attitude will change your results. Attitude is the great multiplier. To multiply positive results, choose positive attitudes.

I can hear you saying, "But Coach, if most of my attitudes have been with me since I was five years old, what can I do about it?"

And that's a great question, because it's not as easy as just deciding you're going to have completely different attitudes from this moment on. You have a complex neural network in your brain that likes you just the way you are. Just as you have to work hard if you want to change your body, you have to work hard to change your mind.

From the time you were a little kid, you got a lot of messages drilled into you, and one of the very first words you learned was "No!" You learned not to answer the door when your parents weren't home. You learned that you weren't allowed to do certain things. You learned never to talk to strangers. The messages mostly came from your parents and were meant to keep you safe. The problem is, you were such a great learner that you really got those messages down cold, and nobody ever mentioned that some of them don't apply in adulthood. Think about it: how far are you going to get in your professional life if you never talk to a stranger?

Changing your attitude starts with recognizing how the world is different now. Just the same way you've adapted away from audio cassette tapes and typewriters to MP3s and a laptop, you need to adapt to a world that is abundant instead of scarce. The world is full of opportunities, not just problems. While other people are fighting over slices of a small pie, you can decide to get out there and make the pie bigger. If you make the conscious decision to see the opportunities and the abundance, you will likely find that stuff was there all along.

It takes work, though. All those negative attitudes got installed by constant repetition. You heard those messages over and over and over again. If you want to get those old messages out of your head and replace them with better ones, you will have to repeat the better messages at least as many times as you heard the old ones. It might take twenty or a hundred or a thousand repetitions of your new belief before it becomes as ingrained as that old stuff. But do you think it might be worth the trouble?

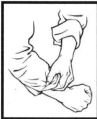

ROLL 'EM! Attitude Overhaul

Pick one, or at most two, attitudes to replace some old ones that aren't working for you. Your new attitudes should describe the person you want to become, in a very concrete way. A good attitude statement has three important elements:

It's in the first person. It's about *you*, not about other people, externalities, or anything you don't directly control. Start your statement with "I am—" or "I can—" or "I believe—." This helps make sure you're keeping it personal.

It's in the present tense. It's about *now*, not about the past or some distant future. Notice that it's "I am" and "I can," not "I will" or "I did" or "I wish." You're describing the person you want to be as if you already are that person, and using the attitude statement to make the dream come true.

It's about the best possible reality, not about limitations or fantasies. Describe yourself as you want to be and as you believe you can be. Most people can't be an NFL star quarterback or a fairy princess; but just about anybody can be a strong leader, a loyal friend, a successful businessperson, or a loving parent. What can you be?

Your best results will come if you write your own attitude statements, but here are some examples to get you thinking:

- I can make new friends by talking to strangers.
- I am a trusted friend.
- I believe I can run the Boston Marathon.

Once you have your new attitudes, write them on several sticky notes and put them where you will see them every day—on your steering wheel, your bathroom mirror, the front door, your desk, your computer monitor—wherever they need to be to make sure you start getting that repetition. Every time you see one of your notes, read it out loud (you can do this quietly if you're afraid your co-workers will think you're nuts). Give this about thirty days—that's how long experts say it takes to create a new habit. At the end of thirty days, evaluate. What's different now from the way it was a month ago? Repeat as necessary until you have attitudes that help you rather than get in your way.

As you go through your life listening to the different messages that come to you, you develop beliefs about yourself and about the world. Beliefs are a little bit different from attitudes (more on that later).

> "Pray as if everything depended on God. Work as if everything depended on you."
>
> —St. Augustine

Think for a minute about the people you have listened to in your life, and what beliefs you have learned from them. Do you have any beliefs that you just accepted without any question? Do you have the exact same religious or political beliefs as your parents, or did you hear things during the course of your life that caused you to question their beliefs and form your own? What about your beliefs about who you are? Do you believe everything other people say about you? Do you believe what you say about yourself?

Ultimately it is your belief in yourself—in your skills, your talent and your uniqueness—that will set you apart from the pack. It's also your belief system. Call it beliefs, core values, spirituality or religion, or just convictions. Your beliefs are essential to who you are and how you show up in the world. What do you believe to be true? What do you believe in? What is core to you as a successful person?

I have a favorite story about belief. It's an old story; maybe you've heard it. It's about a guy named Michael.

~~~

Michael was the kind of guy you love to hate. He was always in a good mood and always had something positive to say. When someone would ask him how he was doing, he would reply, "If I were any better, I would be twins!"

He was a natural motivator. If an employee was having a bad day, Michael was there telling the employee how to look on the positive side of the situation. His style always made people curious, so one day a friend of his asked him, "I don't get it! You can't be a positive person all of the time. How do you do it?"

Michael replied, "Each morning I wake up and say to myself, 'You have two choices today. You can choose to be in a good mood, or you can choose to be in a bad mood.' I choose to be in a good mood. Each time something bad happens, I can choose to be a victim, or I can choose to learn from it. I choose to learn from it. Every time someone comes to me complaining, I can choose to accept their complaining, or I can point out the positive side of life. I choose the positive side of life."

"Yeah, right, it's not that easy," his buddy protested.

"Yes, it is," Michael said. "Life is all about choices. When you cut away all the junk, every situation is a choice. You choose how you react to situations. You choose how people affect your mood. You choose to be in a good mood or bad mood. The bottom line: It's your choice how you live your life."

Several years later, Michael was involved in a serious accident, falling some sixty feet from a communications tower. After eighteen hours of surgery and weeks of intensive care, Michael was released from the hospital with rods placed in his back. The same friend ran into Michael about six months after the accident. When he asked him how he was, he replied. "If I were any better, I'd be twins. Wanna see my scars?"

The friend declined that invitation, but he did ask him what had gone through his mind as the accident took place.

"The first thing that went through my mind was the well-being of my soon-to-be-born daughter," Michael replied. "Then, as I lay on the ground, I remembered that I had two choices: I could choose to live, or I could choose to die. I chose to live."

Michael continued, "The paramedics were great. They kept telling me I was going to be fine. But when they wheeled me into the ER and I saw the expressions on the faces of the doctors and nurses, I got really scared. In their eyes, I read, 'He's a dead man.' I knew I needed to take action."

"What did you do?" the friend asked.

"Well, there was a big burly nurse shouting questions at me," said Michael. "She asked if I was allergic to anything. 'Yes,' I replied. The doctors and nurses stopped working as they waited for my reply. I took a deep breath and yelled, 'Gravity!' "

Over their laughter, I told them, "I am choosing to live. Operate on me as if I am alive, not dead."

Michael lived, thanks to the skill of his doctors, but also because of his amazing attitude. We can learn from Michael that every day we have the choice to live fully. Attitude, after all, is everything.

~~~

What choice do you make when you wake up in the morning? What choices do you make throughout your day, and how are they working for you? Does Michael's approach to life sound too good to be true? Does it sound so ridiculous that you don't even want to try it? What would happen if you tried it anyway?

Attitudes and beliefs are similar. They both drive how you perceive the world and how you act in it. One of the key differences is that beliefs tend to be more conscious. You have a lot of attitudes that you developed early in life, and they color your world in ways you largely don't even notice. Beliefs have more intention than that.

If I tell you it's okay to talk to strangers now that you're an adult, you may not even realize until that moment that you had an outdated attitude about that. You look at me as though I'm some kind of mental case and say, "Well, *duh*, Coach, of *course* it's okay to talk to strangers." But your attitude may unconsciously hold you back from actually doing it—from making cold calls, getting up on stage, or even just striking up a conversation at the grocery store—because the attitude runs so deep.

Beliefs, on the other hand, are something you carry very consciously. Your political views, ethics, morals, and religious or spiritual views are made up of beliefs. You have beliefs about yourself—some positive, some negative—and beliefs about the other people in your life. You believe in your kid's soccer team. Beliefs may or may not be facts, but for you, they are the truth. A belief is an opinion combined with a deep conviction. Many of your beliefs help you, and some of them hurt you, just as your attitudes do. When you fine-tune your beliefs to be supportive of who you are and who you want to be, they will support you and help you support others.

ROLL 'EM! Get Un-Limited

Take out a piece of paper and set it in front of you the wide way. Draw lines to divide it into three columns. In the first column, write down some self-limiting beliefs you have had up to this point in your life. Examples would be things like, "I can't remember names" or "I'm no good at math" or "I'll always be stuck doing this job I hate." Dig deep and be honest—you may have some very strong beliefs about yourself that, when you actually say them out loud, make you really uncomfortable. And like attitudes, some of them may be so deeply held by now that you rarely think about them. Let's get them out where we can take a look.

My old beliefs	How they have NOT served me	How they have NOT served others

Now in the second column, describe how each belief has *not* served you. If you believe, for example, that you're not good at remembering names, your "proof" comes every time you forget a name. But you never notice when you *do* remember a name, so you can't ever reward or appreciate yourself for doing well when it happens. Feeling like a failure doesn't serve you very well, does it?

In the third column, describe how your beliefs do *not* serve others. If you believe you are not good at math, you won't help your son with his math homework, even if it's something you can probably do very well. You've left him in the lurch and lost an opportunity to spend quality time with him. That doesn't serve either of you.

Sit with this information for a bit, then write up some beliefs that *do* serve you and others. If you like, you can use the same three-column process. Write the new belief, describe how it will serve you well, and describe how it will serve others well. Then use the same sticky-note process for these new beliefs that you used with the new attitudes in the previous exercise.

Listening is going to help you discover your purpose. It's always been there—you are here for a reason. The challenge is to uncover it and let it drive everything you do from that moment on. Once you find it, it all comes full circle. Knowing your purpose will give you clarity about what the best work is for you to do, what attitudes and beliefs are going to serve you best, and what actions you need to take to be the best *you* that you can be.

When you understand your purpose, you can learn what you need to learn and live what you need to live. Finding your purpose provides the meaning and the motivation for everything you do.

A person without purpose is floating aimlessly like a buoy in the ocean with no anchor. When you see a buoy, you know it's anchored. A person with no purpose has no anchor and just floats in whatever direction the wind is blowing. People with no purpose can't be a defining point for themselves or anyone else in their lives. Without purpose, you could be a duke, a diplomat, a doctor, or a dog walker and it wouldn't make any difference to you. Any job, any relationship, any life is as good as any other.

A person with purpose is driven. When you have clarity in your purpose, you know what kinds of work are a good fit and which ones are not. You know what kinds of friends you want to have, how you want to spend your time, and what beliefs and attitudes best serve your purpose. Over time, your entire life comes to revolve around the things that are most important to you, and it's easy to jump out of bed in the morning with a great attitude about your day.

To discover your purpose, you have to listen. Listen to yourself, to others, to the lessons of your experience, and to God. Listen to your heart. Psalm 46 says, "Be still and know that I am God." Whatever your beliefs, the purpose for which you are put on this earth will be revealed to you, if you can be quiet enough to hear it. I know you're busy. We're all busy. But what are you busy doing? Are you busy living your life to the limits of your potential, or are you just busy paying the bills and watching television? Try turning off all the "busy" for awhile, and listen to what comes out of the silence.

> Be still and know that I am God.
>
> —Psalm 46

Destiny

Destiny is something we all wonder about. What is it? What will it be? Is it preordained? Most importantly, can we alter it? Destiny is what you choose it to be. Regardless of your belief system from a spiritual or religious perspective, your destiny is your own and no one else's. You are in control of it. If you see you are heading down a path that doesn't fit your vision of who you want to be or what you need and want from your life, it is your responsibility to change direction. Each of us has the power to alter our destiny.

No one else can change your destiny. It is all you! The first step, and the biggest challenge, is to decide what your destiny will be. Once you have clarity in your purpose and begin to set goals related to that, you are well on your way to choosing your destiny.

The second step is accepting that you have the potential to be great—to be the best. Accepting that you can be the best, and deciding to become the best you can be, is a major commitment. Being the best is not a "sometimes" thing; it is a thing you strive for all the time. It is not a part-time job. It is a full-time job. Successful people are those who consistently do what it takes to be great. They do the right things, all the time. Not a few of the right things some of the time, but all the right things all the time. No excuses.

So make the choice! Say yes to greatness, and move toward becoming great. There is incredible power in the commitment once you have made it. It gets into your heart and psyche and it becomes a part of you. Commit to excellence in whatever you choose to do, and greatness will be your reward.

The Price of Success

We all know nothing in this world is free, and we're all concerned about what things cost these days. You may find yourself asking questions such as, "Is my dream worth the cost? Am I willing to pay the price for success?"

Here's a better question (a bunch of them, actually): Is your dream clear? Is your definition of success clear? Do you have clarity in what you want to do? What is your purpose? Your purpose is your great calling—what you are supposed to be doing with your life. Your "God-given purpose" is what some will call it. Even if you haven't figured it out yet, it still is what it is. Your purpose is real and is part of who you are destined to be. When you look at it that way, you may realize that the price of *not* pursuing it is a lot higher than the price of going for it.

Far too often we stop at "I'm okay; life's pretty good here," and lose that drive toward our purpose. When I hear someone say, "I'm okay" or "I'm fine," what I am really hearing is "I'm comfortable." As a coach, my job at that point (as I see it) is to dig deeper. Is this client really okay with where they currently are? (Most are not.) If not, why would they accept okay and not great?

I've heard "it's hard—it's too hard, Coach! I want more but it has just gotten too hard." Now the reality is that it is the "hard" that makes it great! If you want success, however you define it, you will have to work hard, very hard. That alone will help you take a step closer to success—give it all you've got, give it your best and work toward success, as you know it.

When I work with clients, I frequently challenge them on their purpose. Some know right away. Some aren't sure but think they are heading there, others have absolutely no clue. Others just don't really care. They are in the "vacation" mode. They have checked out and hit the ROAD—Retired On Active Duty!

When I find those who think they know or even say they are clear, it's time for me to challenge them. I challenge their assumptions and I challenge their thoughts and beliefs. Is what you are doing really your calling? Is it your true purpose and are you fulfilled?

Everything has a cost to it. The cost might be money, time, energy, relationships, or a combination of those things. The cost varies with each endeavor. There are three kinds of costs: the initial cost, the daily cost, and the cost of regret.

Do you know the initial cost of what you want? The up-front cost is usually about making a change. Sometimes you need to spend some money; other times it's time or energy. Supposing you wanted to start working out. You might need to buy a gym membership, or you might need to haul that old exercise equipment out of the basement (that stuff you bought the last time you decided to start working out). You may have to drop some of your current commitments, hobbies, or habits to make room for the new thing you want to do.

For example, beyond the money investment, getting your master's degree is going to take ten to twenty hours a week or more out of your life. What are you going to take off the calendar to make that time? Ask yourself, "Am I willing to pay the initial cost to achieve what I want? Is it worth it?" If you can answer, "Yes," then you can consider the daily cost.

Day in and day out there will be a cost. What is it and can you pay it? For me the cost of sharing this book with you was long, sometimes sleepless nights and Saturdays spent writing down random thoughts, hoping that once they were re-read they would make some sense. It required reading everything I could get my hands on, and time away from my family. For me, that was the price of writing something I knew God had put in my heart to share—the price of happiness for me in fulfilling my purpose in this way. The same will have to happen for you to achieve your big dream. You might have to skip your weekly poker game, your favorite television shows, or your daily Starbucks to make time and money available to put toward your goal.

You may look at the initial cost and daily cost of that dream of yours, and think, "Well, that's not even worth it." That could be. Maybe this goal of yours isn't as important as you thought. Or maybe that's just fear talking, or laziness. And that's where you have to consider the third cost—the cost of regret.

Can you accept the cost if you choose *not* to find and follow your purpose? How will you feel if your purpose is never fulfilled? Are you going to look back twenty years down the road and kick yourself for not having taken action today? Is that a cost you can accept?

It is really all about vision and action. You can have one or the other, but you cannot have success or happiness without both.

In the book, The Seed: Finding Purpose and Happiness in Life and Work, there is a great definition of purpose:

"Purpose is our ultimate guidance system that provides us with direction for our lives. Purpose fuels us with passion and this passion gives us confidence and vitality to go after our dreams."

—Jon Gordon

Take the time to learn what your purpose is. The time you spend figuring it out is time you will save in the long run, doing the things that bring you true fulfillment instead of wasting your time on things someone else thinks you should be doing.

ROLL 'EM! Draw a Role Map

You'll need at least an hour of quiet, uninterrupted time to complete this exercise. You will also need a big piece of paper—at least 11x17 (bigger would be better)—and a pen or a marker. If you want to get creative, get pens in a few different colors.

Draw a quick circle, big enough to write in but not huge, in the middle of the paper. (Don't worry if it's not round. It is a thought bubble, not geometry homework.) In that circle, write your life purpose. If you don't know what your purpose is, just leave the circle empty for now, but sketch a little anchor near the edge of the circle to remind you that it is for your purpose.

Next, draw a line out from that circle, and make a smaller bubble at the end of that line. In that bubble, write one of your roles. For example, you are someone's son or daughter, so one of your roles is "son" or "daughter." You may also be a spouse, a parent, an employee, a manager, a church member, a board member . . . you get the idea. Draw lines and bubbles radiating out from your purpose circle for every major role you can think of, making the bubbles bigger for the roles that take more of your time and smaller bubbles for the ones you don't spend as much time doing. Then draw lines and bubbles out from the major roles to represent the smaller "sub-roles" that fall under the major roles, with the same size rules. Are you the head chef of your household? The chauffeur for the kids? Bookkeeper, travel agent, bottle washer, teddy bear surgeon? You probably have dozens of important roles. Include as many as you can think of, including the roles you love and the ones you hate. Leave some room around each bubble for some additional text we'll add in the next step.

Now draw some additional lines and bubbles to represent the major tasks each role requires of you. Think in terms of the activities that take the most time and effort, and list the top three to five tasks for each role. It's not essential that you write down every single thing you do; but, rather to get a flavor for how you spend your time in each of your roles.

When your map is, for the most part, complete, lean back a bit and take a good look at it. Look for patterns and themes. Are the biggest bubbles representative of the things that are most important to you? How are you spending your time? How do you *want* to be spending it?

Consider all the different roles and tasks on your map. Are there any you could stop doing? What about things you're not currently doing that you would like to add? Is there anything you could delegate to somebody else, or that would be such a relief to have off your plate that you'd be willing to hire someone to take care of it for you?

What are you doing that you hate? What do you wish you were doing that is getting sidelined because of something that's less important to you? What are you doing that you love? Are you getting as much time as you want to do that?

Keep adding and make notes, draw lines to make connections, and change things around on your role map until you feel that it represents you accurately. Use different colored pens or markers to cross out things you don't want to be doing or make notes about how to delegate those tasks or roles to others. Draw bigger circles in contrasting colors around things you'd like to be spending more of your time on.

Once that's all done, step back from the map and try to see it on a higher level. See if the truth of your purpose reveals itself. If so, great! Write it in, and then reconsider everything on the map from that perspective. Does having clarity of purpose make it easier to choose which roles and priorities are most important?

If your purpose does not show up right away, that's okay. Keep the map in a spot where you will see it every day. Make notes on it whenever the mood strikes. Over the course of a few days or a few weeks, chances are you'll make some important discoveries about yourself.

In part one of this book, my goal was to give you some information. In return, I asked you to listen for the parts that had value for you. My goal for part two here is to inspire you. Inspiration leads to, and comes from, learning, so your end of the bargain in this part will be to see what you can learn. To start, I want to talk a little bit about learning as a process.

If you're like most people, you've never built a house. (Even if you have, humor me and read the rest of this paragraph anyway.) Let's suppose you decided to build your dream house. Would you start by buying some two-by-fours and nailing them together? Of course not. You'd start by learning. You'd have to find the right piece of land to build on. You'd have to learn about different kinds of houses. You'd have to figure out what you want your dream house to look like, and what shapes, sizes and materials are permitted on the land you choose. Then you'd either have to learn how to draw house plans or hire someone to draw them up for you . . . You get the idea. Nothing is accomplished without hard work, but hard work is a waste of sweat unless you know what you're doing.

You also wouldn't be able to build a house completely by yourself. Even if you were going to build it without anyone else's help, you'd still need building materials that somebody else manufactured and a building permit from the local government. And you wouldn't try to do it without at least reading and studying about how to do it, which means using books and resources that other people created.

A faster and more efficient way to get the job done would be to hire experts for some parts, and teachers for the parts you wanted to learn how to do. This section talks about the other people you need to help you achieve your dreams, how to find them, and how to get the most benefit from their talents.

Remember, the first section was about listening. If you're taking these words to heart, you have been listening to your instinct and to the wisdom the world is trying to give you, and you are discovering your purpose.

As you figure out what the right work is that you need to be doing, you need to make sure you know how to do it. That's learning. In this section we talk about different ways of learning: duplicating others, mentoring and coaching, and goal-setting. The first one is externally driven, the second one is collaborative, and the third one is internally driven. All three are needed for a personal development process, just like the one this book is providing for you. Once you get started, the information in this book will help you achieve everything you want to achieve in your purpose and your life.

From the moment we first come into this world, we are learning by duplicating other people. We learn to speak by mimicking the sounds our parents make. We learn to crawl, then walk, then run—all by doing what we observe others doing. If you pay attention, you can learn almost any skill just by watching and duplicating the actions of someone who does it well.

If you want to be successful, watch and duplicate the actions of people you see as successful. Who do you know who has the level of success you would like to have? What is it about their attitude, confidence, *chutzpah* that you would like to have? What are they doing that you need to be doing? Watch and learn.

Don't stop there. Seek those people out and talk to them. Tell them what you're doing. There's a fine line between an admirer and a stalker. Just so we're clear, you want to be the former, not the latter. But talk to them. Most successful people are more than happy to share at least a few of their success stories and tips, and will be flattered that you see them as being so great. Wouldn't you be?

Success leaves clues.

You will have to make the first move, though. Successful people are busy doing the things that make them successful. They aren't going to help you succeed just because you're standing around basking in their glow. It's up to you to figure out what you want from people you admire, and ask for it.

When I was seventeen, I met a guy who would become one of my most influential mentors, and a lifelong friend. His name is Steven Moreria, and at the time, he was twenty-two years old and a business owner. As a seventeen-year-old high school senior, I had two passions. Sadly, school was not one of them. I cared about football, and I cared about work. I met Steven when I went into the deli he owned to get something to eat. At that time, my mom was Steven's banker. Steven just knew, as soon as I sat down with my two big subs and my chips and my soda to fill up those hollow legs of mine, that I was Sally's son. And the next morning when he went to the bank to make his daily deposit, he asked her if I might want a summer job. He's been a great teacher and a great friend ever since.

Steven was all about action. He wasn't very good with details, and when he made a deposit at the bank, it was literally a paper bag full of cash, checks, and receipts—no deposit slips, not even a paper clip. You could do that back then, and for Steven it meant he could chase his dreams without sweating the small stuff. I admired his energy, his drive, and his willingness to take a risk and just flat out go for it. I followed his lead and worked hard to become more like him. A few years later he and I bought a business together and had great success. (That story is coming up in a later chapter.)

Another great role model for me was a guy named Glenn. He was my boss at the first "corporate" job I ever held. Glenn hired me because I was a good salesman, and when he saw me working hard and showing potential, he promoted me. I ended up as a regional manager with responsibility for eight salespeople across six networks in fourteen states.

I started looking for ways to be in meetings with Glenn. I went to lunch meetings with Glenn and the other managers, and swallowed up all the knowledge and information I could get, right along with the greasy burgers we'd eat at those lunches. I heard about pending contracts, potential deals, and ideas for market expansion. I learned the meaning of terms I'd never heard before and had to look them up when we got back to the office.

I learned by watching Glenn how to "manage up" and to act like you already are the person you want to become. Glenn taught me to listen, learn, and exhibit the traits I saw in the people who were doing what I wanted to do. He taught me to watch others closely, to see how they acted in meetings, how they dressed, and how they made decisions. His advice was pure gold to me, and in return, I would tell him, from my perspective, what our division of the company needed to do to grow. I learned to take ownership, look at the big picture, and see the company through the eyes of a CEO. The more I acted like the boss, the more responsibility I was given. By modeling my own actions after the people above me in the food chain, I eventually became one of them.

People who are already successful have worked hard and made mistakes along the way. They can help you avoid the mistakes they made, and help you figure out which hard work is the right hard work. You're going to make mistakes, but maybe they don't have to be the same ones other people have already made. By watching, learning from, and emulating successful people, you can benefit from their experience and skip straight to the really interesting and unique mistakes that only *you* can make. Plus, duplicating others is a method of learning that you've been using all your life, so it will feel easy and natural to do.

There are some caveats to what I'm saying here. Duplicating someone you see as successful does not mean trying to be that person, and it matters what you emulate. Have you ever met somebody who was trying so hard to be someone else that the person totally lost who he or she was? Maybe you even did that. It's a national pastime in middle school and high school. Check out the captain of the football team and the cheerleading squad, and look for all the other people who dress like them, talk like them, put the same pictures up in their lockers, and don't really understand why they aren't popular like the people they are copying.

Duplicating people you admire is not about wearing the same brand of suit or driving the same kind of car. It's about watching how they carry themselves and how they treat other people. It's about seeing how they set their priorities and how they spend their time. Truly successful people are confident and comfortable in the choices they make. There are plenty of successful people driving beater cars and wearing off-brand suits—they just have different priorities. Copy the behavior, not the appearance, of people you admire. Remember that the goal is to be the best *you* that you can be, not the best carbon copy of someone else.

ROLL 'EM! Copycat

Look for people you admire. They could be famous, or just someone in your everyday life you have seen doing things you would like to be able to do. Identify those things they are doing that make them attractive to you—I don't mean attractive looking, so much as attractive in actions. (This is the *action* section!) It may be the way they act or the way they talk to others or how they respond to certain situations. Why did they catch your attention? What is it that makes you want to be more like them? Write down the traits you see that you want to emulate in your own life. Write down stories or examples of how those traits show up in others.

What actions do you need to take to become more like the person(s) you admire? Maybe you have to take a look at where you are now. You're living your life in a certain way right now. How's it working for you? How do you measure up to your heroes? Take out your journal (you do have it close by, right?) and write out two or three things that you would like to duplicate from those people you admire. What are they doing consistently that is positive, that if you do the same thing, it will move you toward your own goals?

Decide how these two or three things need to be applied to your life. How will you turn them into habits? What will be different when you do? For the next thirty days, make a very conscious effort to do these new behaviors. Remember, it takes about thirty days to lock in a new habit, so give yourself about a month to get the hang of the new you, and have patience if you don't get it perfect right away.

Remember, I said back in the first part of the book that most people think negatively, and during the course of your life you collect a lot of "proof" that the world is a horrible place. This is where we're going to do some focused work to change that.

Every night during the month, write down in your journal one short example or story of something you did right toward changing your behavior to be more like the people you admire. You want to catch yourself being good. Part of becoming who you want to be is believing you are that person, and the best way to prove to yourself that you are that person is to have a bunch of examples that show it.

As my friend and fellow coach Doug Brown likes to say, "If you were accused of being the person you most want to be, would there be enough evidence to convict you?" Well, by the end of this book I'm going to accuse you of greatness, so you better start building your case.

Name	Trait or Behavior	My Action

If we were able to do it all in our business, completely on our own, we would all be very successful. That's obviously not the case, neither is this how it works. We have been coached, taught, and mentored since our very beginning by parents, teachers, and other adult role models. We didn't often get to choose those people, and not all of them set a very good example, but we definitely learned from all of them.

Now that we are adults, we get to choose our coaches and mentors, and we can find people who do set consistently good examples for us to follow. Better yet, we can get help from people who are true professionals and experts in the art of coaching.

Here are four reasons why coaching is essential:

1. Coaching is a sure way of learning. When you are being coached by someone who has been there and done that, the person is able to teach you the peculiarities that you can't get by "book learning" alone. Experience is the difference. Using stories and examples, a coach can help us to open our eyes to what our true needs are. We can learn through the eyes of a person who has already made the mistakes and found the most effective way for us to get where we want to go. By learning through a coach we trust, we get a more thorough learning experience and become effective by learning in a manner that shows us the most important action steps for us to achieve success.

2. Coaching is a more effective way to accomplish your goals. With a coach, you have someone who will guide you step by step in your journey to success. A coach will help you to focus on what's important and exactly what you need to do to move forward. A coach will cut out the fluff and get straight to the heart of your success. A good coach can cut years off the learning curve.

3. Coaching gets out of the "books" and uses the power of real-life experience. We live in a world where formal schooling and education is valued, sometimes more than experience. But there is no substitute for real-world experience.

Take driving, for example. If we measured competence in the ability to pass the class or the written test, then every sixteen-year-old would be an expert driver. We all know this is not the case. A driver with years of road experience is a much more proficient driver. This is the reason you need a coach. A coach can see the turns and twists in the road, then help you to see them and navigate them yourself. When you work with a coach, you'll use your own daily experiences as the "workbook." This increases *knowledge transfer* (taking the book concept and putting it into practice in your life) and helps you use more of your skills and talents to achieve your goals.

4. Coaching is a model you can use to "pay it forward." Once you have been coached, your desire to help others will naturally increase. A coach is there for you; his or her focus is on your success and nothing else. Once you see and reach new levels of success, you will begin to notice other people seeking the same thing. Seekers in need of a coach will become apparent to you. This opens the door for you to help them get more from their lives. The Bible says that iron sharpens iron and two working together are stronger that one. Coaching is the secret ingredient of the top performers in business and sports. Michael Phelps, Tiger Woods—these guys are two of the best in the world and it might not look like they need a coach, but they *have* coaches, and that's *why* they are so successful!

Do you want a coach or do you need a mentor?

What is the difference? The difference is *huge*! Both are essential to helping you move forward, to getting you closer to where you want to be. So let's define the difference.

A *mentor* is defined as a trusted counselor or guide. A mentor gives help and advice during a period of time and often acts as a teacher. Mentors have already done what you are planning or hoping to do, and are willing to help you learn the ropes of a particular business or area of knowledge. A mentor is often vested in your success and will usually be someone you have worked with in the past, such as a former co-worker, teacher, or boss. Mentors don't generally go through any special training or certification to become mentors, and the relationship may not be formal. You might not even think of someone as a mentor at the time he or she is mentoring you, but when you look back later in your life you'll realize that "he [or she] sure gave me a leg up when I was new here."

A *coach,* on the other hand, is a professional who uses some type of structured process to help clients maximize their potential. Life, business, and executive coaches work with clients in all areas of their lives, and there are specialty coaches such as career coaches and finance coaches who just focus on one specific area of the client's life. Coaches believe their clients already have the knowledge to achieve their goals, so they just need to draw out the clients' resourcefulness and confidence to get the results they want. Because the coach sees the client as the "expert," coaches are always on the client's agenda, focused on whatever goal or outcome the client has chosen.

If you're ready to get some focused help to get where you want to go, it's time for a coach. Mentors are awesome, and deserve the gratitude of all the newbies they have helped along the way (including you, if you have been lucky enough to have a mentor). But mentors can only take you so far, and usually only in the domain where they have experience. It's also great to watch and duplicate the actions of successful people, and that will help you. But you can't watch what they do every minute of the day, or see inside their heads, and anyway you wouldn't want to. (Remember what I said about stalkers?) To be the best *you* that you can be, you're going to need the kind of help you will find all around you. And that's where a coach comes in.

Coaches support you and they help you to hold you accountable. They are the objective voice who will listen to you, challenge you, and guide you. When you talk to people who have achieved top-shelf success, you're going to find that almost all of them use at least one coach, and a lot of them use more than one.

Are you Coachable?

Before you can be a successful coaching client, you need to be very clear on three things. So ask yourself these three questions, and think hard about your answers:

Am I willing to be totally honest with myself?

Am I willing to change?

Am I ready to put in the time and effort and hard work that will be needed for me to change?

If you can't answer all three of those questions with a confident and unwavering *yes*, you may not be coachable right now. So now ask yourself question number four.

What would it take for me to be able to answer *yes* to all of those questions?

Find Your Coach

For the sake of argument, let's assume you are ready for a coach. How do you find one? You get out into the world and you *look*. You must go and find them because they are *not* looking for *you*! You must make the effort to get the help you need. Look for a specific person who can help you reach new levels of success.

Coaches tend to use one or more of five basic coaching styles: The drill sergeant, the cheerleader, the friend, the expert, and the inquisitor. Sometimes one good coach can be all of these things; other times you might need different coaches to play these different roles. It may be that one of these styles really turns you off, or is exactly what you need. Think about which styles of coaching are most likely to help you achieve your goals, and when you talk to potential coaches, interact with them for long enough to see which of the styles they use.

Drill Sergeant: This is the coach who is going to hold you accountable. A lot of professional coaches who fit this type are literally ex-military guys or former athletes. They are not going to be nice to you. They're going to push you to your limits and beyond them. They will kick your butt when it needs kicking. They can be inspiring, especially if you're someone who wants to do a lot and gets bogged down with procrastination or self-limiting attitudes. If you are slacking and you know it, a drill sergeant is a good coach for you.

Cheerleader: This is the coach who is going to be encouraging and supportive of you and will help you keep your energy up. Some sports coaches (and cardio dance instructors) are like this. They are great to talk to when you are feeling discouraged, because they will remind you that they believe in you and will help you find your excitement and motivation again. They can help you see the bright side of a bad situation, look forward to all the good things that will happen when you achieve your goals, and keep your spirits up no matter what.

The only downside to a cheerleader is that they may not always remember to hold you accountable. Support is great, but if there's no accountability, all that support may allow you to become complacent with where you are.

Friend: This is the coach who is going to listen to you and be like a mirror. They will reflect back what you are saying, and help you notice where you are holding yourself back. This coach will support you and encourage you to reach higher levels of success. A friend type of coach is good for someone who might not be ready to turn his or her entire life upside down, but needs to make changes a little bit at a time. Watch out, though—your actual friends don't always make the best coaches, because they won't be straight with you if they think it will hurt your feelings. A good friend-type coach is still going to be honest and is still going to hold you accountable. This type of coach will still call you on your attitude and your behavior if you're not doing what you need to do. He or she will just do it more gently.

Expert: This is the coach who knows the ins and outs of a particular thing. Sometimes these folks will show up as area-specific coaches, such as a money coach, a fitness coach, or a career coach. In addition to coaching you on behaviors, goal-setting, or whatnot, these coaches can also help you with financial planning, business strategy, or whatever particular area they know. An expert can be a real help if you're new to something, or if you don't have the knowledge you need to achieve some of your goals.

Make sure you understand whether the person you're dealing with is a coach or a consultant, though. Consultants will tell you how to do things. Coaches will to assist you to do what *you* want to do, offering their technical expertise only when it's needed to help you figure things out for yourself.

Inquisitor: This is the coach who can draw from your experience. His or her belief is that you have the answers to your challenges inside you and with the proper questions and exercises you will be able to uncover and use more of your potential. The Inquisitor coach will help you to uncover the real issues by using specialized questioning skills that will allow you to make clear decisions and take action to achieve your goals. Inquisitor-type coaches are your partners or allies in becoming the person you want to be. The inquisitor asks tough questions and listens in a non-critical and non-judgmental way while holding you accountable and challenging you to take the actions necessary to reach your full potential.

Get Engaged

No, I'm not talking about falling on one knee with a big diamond. I mean, once you find the right coach, engage him or her. Get the coach on your team. Do whatever you need to do to get the coach's commitment to help you. If you have to, *hire a coach*! Start the dialog, set a time to talk, establish goals with the person, and take action.

Once you have engaged your coach or mentor, it is up to you to utilize him or her. If you are paying the coach, get your money's worth. Use the coach's time, experience, and knowledge. You got the coach engaged, now you need to get yourself engaged. Take advantage of everything your coach or mentor has to offer. If you're working with someone who is just helping you out of the goodness of his or her heart, though, take care not to overuse him or her. If you need to meet with your coach, buy lunch. Find ways to return the kindness given to you. Give more than you get and you will reap the rewards.

Using a coach properly is critical for get the results you want. Coaching is one of the fastest growing professions and most talked-about movements in business today. New business coaches, executive coaches, team coaches, and life coaches are hanging out their shingles every day. There are articles daily that tout the need for, and value of, having a coach work with you. Managers, leaders, and employees at all levels are becoming more productive and reaching higher levels of success by employing a coach to help keep them on track.

Coaching is much different from consulting. A coach does not focus on telling a client what to do; but rather, helps clients see what they know has to be done and holds them accountable to take the necessary action. Coaches aren't there to fix you or solve your problem as much as they are there to be an objective sounding board for you, the client. The coach will work to help you to learn and develop the necessary skills that are necessary to allow you to reach your goals. He or she will be a supporter for you and will look at how you are approaching the issue, challenge, or problem all the while helping you realize the right action to take. A good coach is always on *your* agenda.

While the profession of coaching is relatively new in its current form, the model has been around since the beginning of time. Think of the term mentor. The first thing that comes to my mind when I hear that word is the old '70's show *Kung Fu* with David Carradine who played Kwai Chang Caine, a Shaolin priest. In one famous scene, Caine spoke with Master Po:

Master Po: "Fear is the only darkness. Never assume that because a man has no eyes, he cannot see. Close your eyes. What do you hear?'"

Caine: "I hear the water. I hear the birds."

Po: "Do you hear your own heartbeat?"

Caine: "No."

Po: "Do you hear the grasshopper which is at your feet?"

Caine opens his eyes and looks down at his feet to see a grasshopper there. "Old Man, how is it that you hear these things?"

Po: "Young Man, how is it that you do not?"

Master Po and others served as Caine's coaches by helping him to see, hear, and accomplish things that were already there but because of outside influences he could not yet see or do them.

This is the role of today's coach—to help you see the things that are there but are hidden because of outside influences, old habits, paradigms, or beliefs you have.

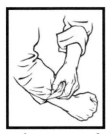

ROLL 'EM! Get a Coach

Are you ready for a coach? If so, it is up to you to find one. Get out your journal or a notepad and write down the qualities you want in your coach. List five to six personal qualities that would make a coach a good fit for you. Think about how you are best motivated. What is the best way to get you going? Is it with someone who has an authoritarian style, the drill sergeant type? Do you need encouragement or a cheerleader type? Or do you want someone who will ask you to challenge yourself and help you uncover your deepest, darkest fears—the one who can peel back all your layers of defense and get to the heart of the matter?

No matter which style or qualities you want in a coach, define them. Then, start to interview coaches. Look for a connection, a level of comfort with the coach. The right coach might have twenty years of experience or two months. He or she might be older than you or younger. The only thing that really matters is that you feel comfortable with the coach, as though you can really trust him or her. Trust is key! Don't be afraid to interview as many coaches as you need to until you find the right one. Then, *hire him or her!* Make the commitment and get to work!

So here are the three concrete steps to take to find a coach:

Decide what kind of coach you want and need.

Interview coaches to find the right fit.

Make a decision, take action, and hire your coach.

Do you allow yourself to be held accountable for your actions on your commitments? How do you keep track of them? Who is your accountability partner? Your boss will hold you accountable, but by the time your boss is asking about it, it's already too late. Expecting your boss to be your only source for accountability is a scarcity tactic—it puts you on a negative footing where you are depending on external "carrot and stick" factors to motivate you.

Instead, find a peer who can partner with you. The best way to be held accountable is to be someone's accountability partner. Who will you hold accountable, who will also hold you accountable? It should be someone you trust, who is close enough to your situation to help you work through challenges and far enough away to be objective about them.

Are you clear about what commitments you have made? Have you shared your commitments with your team, your boss, and your peers? Do you communicate regularly about how you are doing and what you need for success?

Accountability isn't just about being kicked in the butt and pushed to get the work done. It's also about getting help and support from others. Too often we fear we are showing weakness when we ask for help or say we are struggling. Bull hockey! We show strength when we are able to recognize where we need help. Imagine if an army platoon in the heat of a battle never communicated that they were struggling on a particular front. What would happen? Nobody's going to be thanking Sergeant Tough Guy for being too proud to say he needed help when he, his guys, and the whole platoon are lost. The people who are counting on you don't want you to be a martyr—they want you to be a success. Ask for help when you need it.

Evaluate

Practically every word you've ever read about personal growth and development uses the term journey as a metaphor for working toward success, right? Well, that's because it's a good metaphor, and it works especially well when we talk about evaluation. If you're going somewhere you haven't been before, such as a new level of success, you need a map. And before a map will help you, you have to know where you are. And that's not only true at the very beginning of your journey—it's true every step of the way. So you need to be constantly evaluating where you are.

How are you doing with respect to your goals? Have you set your goals and expectations for yourself? In order to evaluate anything, you have to have standards set—basically that's your map showing your destination. It lets you evaluate how far away you are from it. You have to know where you want to end up if you ever want to get there. Far too many times people say they want to "improve, grow, succeed," blah, blah, blah. Well, great. That's like saying, "I want to go on vacation to somewhere beautiful." Call your travel agent and tell her (or him) to book you a ticket to "somewhere beautiful." I guarantee you the agent will want you to be more specific. Just what do you want to be, have, do, become, see, live like? Whatever your end point is, what is it? What, specifically, does your life look like to you?

We all are driven by the desire to avoid pain and increase pleasure.

Let's talk about Blue Bell® ice cream. I love my Blue Bell at night. For a long time, I loved it *every* night. Up until I couldn't fit into my favorite jeans. Then the pain of not fitting into my favorite jeans overrode the pleasure of the Blue Bell. Did I enjoy cutting out my Blue Bell? No way. But it hurt me more to be straining the button on my jeans than it did to cut back on the ice cream. Change often hurts, and that's why we will never change our habits until it hurts less to change than it hurts to stay the same. Working out is a perfect example. I would rather sit on the couch watching television and eating that Blue Bell, or stay in bed than get up early and go to the gym and run or work out. Change is uncomfortable. Change is scary. And change is inevitable. How you handle it is going to determine how, and even if, you come out the other side. Are you going to get in there and make the change and gain the growth, or are you going to stay stuck where you are?

Good things cannot begin for you until the bad things end. Sometimes we have to throw out some bad to get to the good. We all walk around with some "junk in the trunk," but some people are just plain unhealthy to be around. They may be good enough people in their own right, but just not good for you to be around. They create conflict and pain when they are around you. It might be them, it might be you, it might just be the chemistry between you, but it's no good for you to stick with them. To these people I say, "Go with God, but *go*." Now, you don't have to be ugly about it, just firm and definitive. Don't tell me you've never broken up with somebody before! It's no fun, and nobody likes to do it, but just as you wouldn't stay in a toxic marriage, you can't stay in a toxic friendship or business relationship either. Every day you let a bad relationship continue, it's holding both of you back from becoming your best selves. Trust me—you're doing *both* of you a favor by getting unhealthy relationships out of your life.

Goal-Getting

Goals are critical to success. Without goals you have no point of reference, no direction, no end game. The late great Dr. Stephen Covey taught that we must "begin with the end in mind." Do you know your end game?

Goal-setting is important. Goal-*getting* is key! Accomplishing your goals will make all the difference. Setting your goals doesn't have to be complicated, but it does have to be SMART. The goals that will give you that direction and that end game are SMART: *Specific, Measurable, Attainable, Realistically High, and Time-based.* In other words, define your goals so that you will know, with absolute certainty, how to achieve them and when you have done it.

One of my favorite stories about the power of goal-setting is about Coach Jimmy V—Jim Valvano. I was fortunate enough to play basketball under his guidance at a summer basketball camp in 1975 (more on that later). When Valvano was seventeen years old, he took out a simple white index card and wrote down all of his professional aspirations. He would play basketball in high school and college, become an assistant basketball coach, then a head coach, achieve a victory in Madison Square Garden, and finally cut down the nets after winning a National Championship. Coach Valvano's ability to see his place in the world with such clarity was truly a gift. This simple card, coupled with a strong belief that he could control his fate, would guide the next ten years of his life.

I recently saw a documentary about Jimmy V. I learned that his wife used to talk about "those damn white index cards" that he always carried. He had one in his pocket on the day he passed away. On it he had written his last goal—to find a cure for cancer and beat it. Unfortunately, he didn't beat cancer himself, but the V Foundation, created in his memory, has raised millions of dollars toward finding a cure. You see, when you have that kind of commitment to your goals, you leave a legacy that's bigger than you—even when you are the kind of guy who is bigger than life.

Even if your goals aren't as completely clear or single-minded as Jimmy V's were, you can still write them down, commit to them totally, and take action every day to reach them. What will *your* legacy look like?

On May 6, 1954, Roger Bannister beat the four-minute mile with a time of 3:59.4. Forty-one days later, John Landy broke that record with a 3:57.9. Each runner set the bar a little higher for himself. They challenged their own attitudes about what they thought they could do. They made a commitment to their sport and to being better. Then they went out each day and worked. They took action to achieve their goals. They were immortalized with a bronze statue celebrating their accomplishment.

Most of us won't get a statue, but all of us can roll up our sleeves and accomplish more than we ever thought by challenging our own attitudes and setting the bar a little higher for ourselves. *How are you setting the bar higher for yourself?*

The Power of Goals

I first learned about the power of goals years ago, but at the time I didn't know what or how powerful they were.

Back in about 1988 or so I was going through life without much direction, taking each day as it came. "One day at a time" could have been my motto, if I'd had enough motivation and focus to bother adopting a motto. I was living my life for others. I showed up when I was scheduled, did what I was told to do, and left after things were done. Easy! Maybe you have lived like this sometime in your life. You may even be living like this now.

Well, I was just minding my own business, going through the motions of life, expecting to be told what to do and where to be. Then one day I saw that the local chamber of commerce was putting on a class—a "time management" class. Interesting. Time management. Not anything I had put much thought into up until then. I was intrigued, so I thought, "What the heck, I'll try it." The price was right, the day was right, and I had some time on my hands. Maybe, just maybe, I would get something out of this class.

So I showed up for the class. We were given a thin stack of bound papers—our "workbook"—and we began the class. Now remember, this was the 1980s. I was all about single life, Rock 'N Roll Hair Bands, and fun. I wasn't sure I needed a "workbook," but I acquiesced and decided to give it a shot. The class ran for an entire afternoon and covered a bunch of ideas and information.

I wrote all kinds of things down and learned a little bit about using a day planner (with a *paper binder*—no iPhones or fancy gadgets in 1988!). Then the instructor closed out the class with a short exercise. Looking back, I don't even remember doing this but I know I did, because fourteen years later, as I was cleaning out some of my file cabinets and old boxes of accumulated stuff, I found the workbook. As I started looking through it, I remembered all the subjects we had covered about prioritizing, scheduling, and such. But the biggest a-ha moment was when I got to that last exercise, *goal-setting*.

I have told you all that, to tell you this: I had written down nine goals fourteen years earlier.

One set was short-term, one year or less. The second was mid-length goals, one to five years out, and the third set was longer term, five to fifteen years out. As I started to review and read them, I realized *I had accomplished each of them:*

44

I had been promoted to manager

I had bought my first house.

I had gotten married.

Then:

I had gotten a better job with a big company.

I had started my own company.

I had joined a church.

Finally the long term goals:

I had pretty much accomplished two out of three of those at that time.

This was amazing. But the really amazing thing was that *I had not looked at these goals for almost fourteen years*, yet I had accomplished them! Why? Because I wrote them down, made a commitment to them, and owned them as mine. I was using the SMARTWAY goal process; I just didn't know it at the time.

This is the power of the goals you write down and own. What goals will you commit to: short-term, mid-length, long-term?

Coach Rick's SMARTWAY

The "SMART criteria" for goal-setting have been around since the 1980s. You may have heard them before, even before I listed them earlier.. The SMART criteria are good, but let me give you an example of a SMART goal that's still not that great a goal. Here's the goal: lose ten pounds by July 1. Is it specific? Sure. Is it measurable? You bet. Is it attainable? Let's assume the person whose goal this is has ten pounds he or she could spare, and today is January 15, so yes, it's doable. Is it realistically high? Again, let's give it that for the person in question. Is it time-based? Yes, it has a specific deadline date.

So what's the problem? The problem is that the hypothetical person who wants to do this is currently diabetic, working seventy-five hours a week, a single mom, and has set this goal because her sister told her she looks fat. She hasn't written down her goal and hasn't even thought about how she will achieve it. She has added an extra stressor onto an already crazy life, and there's no way she's going to pull this off.

Another great line from Dr. Stephen Covey is about climbing the ladder of success and finding out it was leaning against the wrong wall. The way to make sure this doesn't happen to you is to set your goals the SMARTWAY. Make them SMART, for sure but also make sure they are *Written* down, *Aligned* with your purpose and the other priorities of your life, and *Yours*.

If our single mom was being totally honest with herself, she would notice that she's avoiding writing her goal down because she's not really feeling it. She's not feeling it because it's not aligned with her needs right now. She already has a heavy work load and a child that are her highest priorities. Trying to think about counting calories or fitting in a workout is just not going to fly for her right now. And most important of all, this goal isn't *her* goal. It's something someone else thinks she should do. She's not bought in. And when—not *if*, but when—she doesn't achieve her goal, she won't even need her sister to say a word about it. She will trash talk herself worse than her sister could ever manage.

Let's drill down on the SMARTWAY of setting goals. The first step is to choose a goal, and I recommend you start with the WAY part rather than the SMART part. Obviously you're going to write it down, so that's the Written taken care of. The next piece is to make sure it's Aligned with your purpose and other priorities. If you look at your role map that you completed previously, you can probably identify some things you want to do differently. Maybe you want to devote more time to one of your roles or less time to another because your life purpose is telling you that parenting is a higher priority than volunteering right now, for example, or you learned in the process of doing your role map, that your faith is important to you, and you want to find a new church home. Whatever goals you choose, make sure they align with your purpose, and make sure you can fit them in with everything else you're doing.

The last, and most important part of WAY is to make sure your goal is really Yours. This is our daily reality—everybody wants a piece of us. In America, many people work well over forty hours a week, get less paid vacation than workers in many other industrialized countries, and don't even take all the vacation they are entitled to. When we get home, there's the laundry, the dishes, the kids, the dog, and whatever obligations we have to our church, our neighborhood association, and civic groups. It makes you tired just thinking about it, right? And odds are you have a list of things you need to do that feels a mile long, mostly to satisfy all those other people. If you intend to be the best *you* that you can be, you may need to let some of that other stuff go so you can focus on what matters most to *you*. Don't make the mistake of thinking a goal is Yours if you're doing it because your boss or your wife or your kid or the president of your Rotary has decided it's important. You can, and you probably do, choose to serve those people, and that's fine and good. But the goals you set for your own development need to be *your* goals, or they will never happen.

Now that we have that all cleared up, let's consider an example goal. And to help it hit home, I'm going to tell you a true story about a real person who set a real goal and used this process to achieve it. The real person is my younger daughter.

Back when my baby girl was just nine years old, she came to me one day with a request. She asked, "Daddy, I need to set a goal."

In my infinite wisdom I said, "Sure honey, what is it?" I figured it would be something like go to the mall or go to the park or something. But to my surprise, she had a BHAG—and she needed some help to plan it.

"Hold up, Coach Rick," you're saying. "What the heck is a BHAG?"

A BHAG is a Big Hairy Audacious Goal—a goal that is out at the edge of what you believe you can do. It's an ambitious, long-term, doozey of a goal. In my daughter's case (and remember, this kid is nine years old), the goal was to save up $100 to buy several items she saw in a catalog.

So we set out to plan her goal. I said, "Let's get some paper and write it down" (using Coach Rick's SMARTWAY process).

She promptly said, "No, Daddy, I want to use one of your special GPS sheets for this one." (Oh yeah, it's rubbing off!)

So we sat down with a GPS sheet (don't worry, I'm going to explain what that is in a couple of paragraphs) and she stated she wanted to make $100 to buy a chair, a lamp, and some girly artwork for her wall from the catalog.

We proceeded to write her goal down using the SMARTWAY criteria. We established she wanted to save $100 by October 31 (Halloween). It was then June 14. She was nine and had a clearly defined goal that was hers and met all the SMARTWAY criteria. She worked through the whole GOSAT process (have patience, all these crazy acronyms will be explained soon) and created a step-by-step plan to achieve her goal. She came up with a plan to ask Mom and Dad to let her do some chores and get paid for them. We agreed on a dollar for taking out the trash, a dollar for picking up her room, and so on.

(I know some of you will push back saying, "Hey, it is her responsibility to keep her room clean and help around the house." I don't care! It was worth a few bucks to me to see her making this plan and negotiating her rewards.)

So she did this all through the summer and into the school year until, on October 12, she came to me and proudly said, "Daddy, I have $104 saved!"

My reply was, "Wow, that is great! Are you ready to get those things you wanted now?"

Her answer was, "No. Now I want to save another $100 because I now want a Nano iPod."

I almost fell off my chair laughing. She had achieved her goal and immediately set a newer, bigger one for herself. My nine-year-old, the latest poster child for the power of goal planning! So my little daughter took the same principles you are seeing in this book and used them to achieve exactly what she wanted.

Here's the big question for you: if a nine year old child can accomplish what she wants using the SMARTWAY GPS system, what can *you* accomplish using it as an adult? How powerful is this to you and how will you put it to use?

The GPS, or "Goal Planning System," is a process, and a worksheet. You'll find a sample one in the back of the book, and you can download full size versions on my website. To fill it out, you're going to use a process that abbreviates to GOSAT: Goal, Obstacles, Solutions, Actions, Time to Implement.

ROLL 'EM! Navigate by GPS

My daughter planned and achieved her goal, and now it's your turn. Flip to the back of the book in the Tools section or go to your computer, download a GPS worksheet from my website (www.CoachRickKolster.com), and print it out. Choose a goal that's on your mind right now, and we'll work through the steps in planning it.

1. Write your Goal. Formulate a goal that meets the SMARTWAY criteria. In order to write a good, clear goal, you'll need to have clarity about what you want. What is the end game? What results do you want to accomplish or achieve? Formulate a SMARTWAY goal, write it down, and start planning.

As you get into the details of planning how to get the results you want, it is important to understand where you are now. Let me give you an example. Supposing you want to try a new restaurant in town that everybody is talking about, but you've never been there. You call the restaurant to ask how to get there. I can promise you the first question they will ask you is, "Where are you coming from?" The only way to know how to get to your goal—to be able to plan it the SMARTWAY—is to understand where you're starting from. Then, once you have your goal clearly defined, you are ready to do the rest of the GOSAT process.

2. Identify Obstacles. The "O" in GOSAT stands for obstacles. Obstacles are the answer to the question, "If this is so important to me, why isn't it already done?" You're not stupid. You're not lazy. You're not a failure. So there must be some good reason why you haven't accomplished this goal yet. Maybe it's because you just graduated from college and your goal is to save $2 million for retirement. So your first obstacle is that you haven't gotten a job yet. Nothing wrong with that, it's just an obstacle you need to clear out of your way so you can get closer to your goal.

The key thing about obstacles is that you want to really think through and write down every single one you can think of. The reason for this is that a lot of times it's the little ones that will trip you up. If your goal is to pay off your mortgage and you can't find your checkbook, that's an obstacle. There's an old saying that goes, "It's not the mountain that wears you down; it's the grain of sand in your shoe." So make sure you write down *all* the possible obstacles that stand between you and your goal—the big ones, such as getting a job, and the little ones, such as finding your checkbook. Then move on to Solutions.

3. Find the Solutions. The "S" in GOSAT is "Solutions." Once you've written out all those obstacles, you may feel a little intimidated about your goal. That's why it's important to get to work on your solutions right away. Look at each obstacle and work out how you are going to overcome it. Some of them, such as getting a job, might require some serious time and effort, while others, such as finding your checkbook, might be little things you could knock out by the end of the day.

Don't be afraid to use your imagination when you think about solutions. Sometimes it can be empowering to brainstorm all the crazy ideas you can think of to solve a problem, and sometimes your craziest idea can turn into a solid solution to your obstacle. Somebody figured out that the horrible bitter berries on an olive tree became a tasty snack if you soaked them in lye, the caustic stuff they use to make soap. What is that about? Well, sometimes the craziest idea becomes a perfect solution to a problem.

4. Take Action. Obviously your bigger obstacles are probably going to have complex solutions that will take more than one step to complete. So the "A" in GOSAT is about ACTION. This is where you work out the exact steps you will need to take to execute your solutions. Each step should be something you can put on your calendar and do. Write your action steps using action words such as: *call, make, go.* Your action steps should clearly define what you need to do so that when you see it on your calendar, you don't think about it, you just do it.

Be sure to reality-check your action steps. Since you have mapped out actions based on solutions that were based on obstacles, you may have ended up with a random bunch of actions you need to take, and they will probably need to be put in some kind of order before you put them on your calendar. If you are saving for retirement, you have to build up some savings before you can invest part of that savings. So make sure your action steps make sense in the order you plan to do them.

5. Give it Time. The last piece of the GOSAT process is the T—Time to implement. This is related to the action steps. Most goals are going to take more than a couple of days to accomplish. In some cases, individual actions could take an entire day, and there might be dozens of actions needed to achieve your goal. In the meantime, life is going on. You still have to go to work, sleep, do the laundry, and pick up the kids from school. The actions related to your goal are only a fraction of all the things you have to do in a day. So it's important to be realistic about how long it's going to take to get it all done. This is where placing your action steps on your calendar pays off—it lets you see them in the context of the rest of your life. You might not be able to work toward your goal every single day, but if your action steps are on your calendar, your goal will stay top of mind for you.

If your goal met the SMARTWAY criteria, you had a target date in it when you first wrote it down. Once you start fitting the action steps into your life, you might discover that the target date you set is too aggressive, or not aggressive enough. Go ahead and change it. It's *your* goal, so make sure it fits your life.

One last thing to do before you roll up your sleeves and get to work on your goal: go back over the list of actions and make sure that you have completed everything that needs to be done. Sometimes there are steps in your goal that don't come straight out of obstacles and solutions. Make sure that the completion of all your action steps actually completes your goal. If anything is missing, get it written down and added to your to-do list.

Live

We've come a long way together already. Thanks for sticking with me through listening and learning. I hope you have some good information and some good inspiration now. In this third part of the book, my goal is to *incite* you to live your best life. Once you understand your purpose and you know how to do the work you need to do, it's time to get on with it—to roll up your sleeves and get to work. Living an on-purpose life is about making a commitment to work hard, play hard, and do whatever it takes to be the best you can be.

Remember my friend and mentor Steven? You met him in the section about duplicating others. Steven says that life is about the next step. It's about being willing to take an extra step beyond what other people are willing to do. Commitment to go above and beyond what is ordinary and expected is the difference between success and failure—between living your best life and just getting by.

In this section, I'll talk about what it really means to make a commitment. Then I'll get into the issue of life balance—keeping all your different roles, priorities, and responsibilities in harmony. Remember the old saying that not one person has ever lain on his or her deathbed saying, "I wish I had spent more time at the office." Even if you love your work (and I hope you do), you won't do your best work if work is all you ever do. Balancing your life with family time, fun time, and taking care of yourself are all important to living your purpose. And sometimes it's just pure luck—so we'll look at some of the ways you can set yourself up to be lucky!

Attitude and knowledge are important, but they won't get you very far without action. Nothing gets done until you *do* it. If you want results, you must take action.

The opposite of action is procrastination. At one time or another we've all procrastinated. All of us have put off something we know we should be doing: the work project we don't really want to do, the laundry, the dishes, taking the dog to the vet. Maybe you've even put off something you wanted to do because you felt guilty about not doing other stuff you were supposed to be doing, and then nothing at all was done.

Why do we procrastinate? There are many reasons. Maybe the goal or the next step is not clear. Maybe we have an attitude problem or we're afraid to start or we haven't really committed. We can't manage our time or make the right choices if we don't make a commitment to the goal and take action.

What commitments have you made in the past

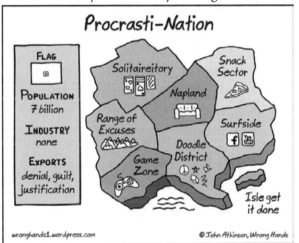

week, the past month, or the past year? How are they going? What actions do you need to take in order to accomplish your goals? What does your to-do list look like? Your to-dos should be directly related to the actions that will lead you closer to accomplishing *your* goals. So first things first—set your goals using the SMARTWAY process. Remember to stay focused on *your* goals—not your sales or budget numbers, not your boss's goals, not your spouse's goals, not the things you think you "should" do, but your own goals aligned with your purpose and values. What do you most want in your life? Is it clear? Is it in writing? Can you explain it to others?

Commitment

Vince Lombardi was famous for beginning every summer training camp with a meeting. This meeting was for everyone. No one was exempt. He began the meeting with these simple words: "Gentlemen, this is a football." He would

> The quality of a person's life is in direct proportion to their commitment to excellence, regardless of their chosen field of endeavor.
>
> —Vince Lombardi

explain the ball and its role in the game and then take everyone outside and show them the field. Moving from sideline to sideline, end zone to end zone he covered the shape, size, and marking of the field. He made a commitment to each of his players that they would understand the "basics" of the game— commitment to know the rules and to master the core competencies of the game. He instilled a sense of commitment to excellence into each of his players. Rookies and Hall-of-Famers were all treated alike.

What is your commitment to excellence? How about a commitment to yourself? Have you made a conscious decision to be the best you can be?

What about the "basics"? When was the last time you really thought about the fundamental rules of the game of your life? Doctors have the Hippocratic Oath. Spouses have their marriage vows. Elected officials have an oath of office. What are your basics? Could you use a review on the role of the ball and the markings on the playing field of your life?

I mentioned Coach Jimmy V in the last section. Let me tell you more about how I knew him.

Back in the '70s when I was a teenager, basketball was my sport. Even though I don't play much these days, it's still my sport—I love that game! Back then I played all the time and even got my parents to send me to camp for a week in 1975. That was where I met Jimmy V.

Coach Jim Valvano was one of the instructors at the Pocono Invitational Basketball Camp. I was a high school sophomore, and I just wanted to be the best. Jimmy V was one of the best already. By this time he had coached at Rutgers, Johns Hopkins, and Bucknell, and now he was head coach at Iona College. By 1979, he would take little Iona College to the NCAA 64 twice. *Wow*!

He had what it took to be an inspiration to so many young men. He had commitment to be the best. That commitment took him and his team to victory in the NCAA National Championship in 1983 with North Carolina State over a huge favorite in Houston with Hall of Fame players Clyde Drexler and Hakeem Olajuwon. (Just in case you thought that index card of his was just for show.)

He had commitment and showed it every day. At camp he would carry a skateboard with a stuffed rat on it. He would tell us to "be a rat." He meant that we needed to become a defensive "rat." We had to be willing to commit to taking a charge foul—to get run over by the driving player who usually had a full head of steam going to the hoop. What did this mean? It meant you were going to get run over. Big time. Every time. But it also meant you had to take a position, make a commitment, and stand your ground, even if it meant getting clobbered. It meant your teammate could count on you to hold your position. He knew you would "take one for the team." Your team could count on your commitment to protect the basket.

Ask yourself this: are you making a commitment? Have you made a commitment to your own success, even when it isn't easy and might get you clobbered?

In team sports like basketball, commitment is both an individual effort and a team effort. Have you ever been on a team that was committed to something, but not every individual on that team was equally committed? Sometimes individuals "come along for the ride" on a team commitment. They are involved, but they are not fully committed.

The best example I ever heard of regarding the difference between involvement and commitment was a story about an old farmer. The farmer lived in one of those great old two-story farmhouses and he raised pigs and chickens. He would say, "You know, sometimes folks don't get the difference between being involved and being committed. Being a farmer is hard work, but these animals of mine take it to a whole different level. You think about breakfast. Eggs and bacon—it takes a lot to put that on your table. I have to raise the chickens, and they have to lay those eggs. But now think about the bacon for a minute. The chickens and I are involved, but the pig is *committed*."

This idea of going beyond involvement on a team to total commitment is key to the success of both the team and each individual member. Let's look at that in a little more depth.

Personal Commitment

In his book, *The 5 Dysfunctions of a Team*, Patrick Lencioni talks about dysfunction number three: lack of commitment. He says that lack of commitment is best overcome by gaining buy-in and achieving clarity. Buy-in is different from consensus or "majority rules." We've all been in a situation where we agreed to something when we weren't fully on board with it. When you're in that situation and it's time to do the work, are you all gung-ho to get it done, or do you just go through the motions? More likely it's the latter, right? Gaining buy-in means not just talking people into something, but having them be fully committed to the direction you're headed. You have to pull out and get rid of all the assumptions and hidden agendas so everyone really understands the goal and can commit to it completely.

Lencioni discusses two techniques for overcoming the "lack of commitment" dysfunction. He calls them *commitment clarification* and *cascading communication*.

Commitment clarification deals with leaders asking: what exactly have we decided here today? This ensures that everyone leaves a meeting with the same impressions. How many times have you come out of a meeting thinking, "Okay, what just happened?" You felt as though the meeting was a total waste of time because no clear decision was made. When the meeting concludes with a clear statement of what decisions were made and who needs to do what next, the work is a lot more likely to get done, and done right.

Do you make a conscious decision and commit to specific actions with your team? Remember, your team isn't just the people you work with, either. Your family is a team. Your friends, the people you do volunteer work with, and even your golf foursome are a team. If you want to get more done and have more fun, make sure everyone on every team you play on is working toward a common goal.

Cascading communication means that the people who made the decisions and committed to the actions in the meeting make sure they communicate that information quickly and clearly to everyone else who might need to know. Employees don't usually eavesdrop on manager meetings, and most folks I know can't read minds. So if you want your people to commit to some course of action, you're going to have to tell them what that course of action would be. People are not like mushrooms—they do not thrive if you keep them in the dark and feed them cow pies. Everyone needs to know what's going on so they can make their best contribution.

All In

Back in the '90's I had a chance to go white water rafting. There were eight of us plus the guide in the boat. We were in Colorado, running the Royal Gorge on the Arkansas River. The river was running strong and we had to navigate Class III and IV rapids. (To give you an idea of what that means, Class V is for pros only, Class VI is nearly impossible, even for experts.) This was an extremely challenging river and at this time of the year it was moving pretty quickly.

The group navigated the morning rapids successfully, and we began to work together pretty well. After lunch we were on to the second half of the river. The rapids we would be paddling in the afternoon included Sunshine Falls (no problem), Sledgehammer (still okay), Wall Slammer (whoa!), and Boat-Eater (oh *no*!).

Well, Sunshine Falls turned out to be 320 cubic feet per second of water raging through a narrow channel—oh, and a thirty-five foot drop. " 'Sunshine, my Aunt Patootie!' " As we started in, the guide yelled out, "Are you all ready?"

"Ready for what?" someone yells back over the din of the falls.

"Ready to take this one on!" came the reply. "I need everyone to be ready to put his paddle in the water and paddle as hard as he can [it was all guys] until we are through the falls. If you stop we may capsize and could get thrown out of the boat and get hurt or even killed! [Huh? *Killed?*] Once we commit, we are all in and must work full out until we are through. Are you ready? Are you all in?"

Well, since I'm not dead, you can guess what my answer was.

What's yours? What do you want out of your life? What are you willing to commit to? *Are you all in?*

Hard Work

Work for a better life for your grandkids, not your own kids.

Too many times the second generation of successful people thinks they have hit a home run when they step into a leadership role in their parents' business. The reality is they were born on third base and made it home. They've probably lived and breathed the business all their lives, and for that very reason, they've never gotten the, "Gentlemen, this is a football," lecture. They didn't have to build it up from nothing, so they probably don't know how. This doesn't make them bad kids, but it also doesn't magically make them great businesspeople.

If the second generation doesn't learn the basics of the business, or if they don't make that "all-in" commitment to excellence and holding up the values and principles that underlie the business, they will burn up or burn out the success of their parents.

Now, inheriting a successful business from my parents was *not* the problem I had to face as a young adult. I bought a business in 1981. I was twenty-two when my buddy Steven and I decided to buy a local pub from a long-term owner. It was the little beer joint where we would go after work and have a beer or ten. We made him an offer and he took it. In case you were wondering, buying a business from a long-term owner is another thing that doesn't magically make you a great businessman!

So now we had this bar—now what? Never having been the type to do anything the easy way, we decided to completely renovate the place. It was a dump, and over fifty years old. It was on the first floor of an old house right on the main drag through town. It took blood, sweat, and tears to get it open. We ripped the entire place apart. All the walls, all the floors—we even dug out the crawl space by hand to make more room for moving beer and bar stock.

For two months, we spent every day digging, carrying out old plywood and plaster, and bringing in new wood for walls and floors. We rebuilt the place top to bottom. In my spare time from the physical labor, I was setting up the bar, kitchen, and menu, learning how to do the books, and hiring staff. I put in about eighteen hours a day.

Every day I was up early, working hard to make sure this place would be ready to open on our big grand opening day. June 30, 1981, was the beginning of the legend of Saints and Sinners in the Valley in West Orange, New Jersey. It was a life's dream, to own my own restaurant/bar, to be a businessman and live my dream. What I didn't know was that this would be the hardest thing I would ever do. It was back-breaking, mind-numbing work. Each day was a new adventure, starting early in the morning and ending in total exhaustion, late at night. I was responsible for everything, from staffing to ordering beer and liquor to food to money handling.

"Wow, Coach," I hear you saying, "sounds rough. Was it worth it?"

You bet it was. Within four months, we were the highest volume seller of Budweiser® products in the county. We were profitable and the place was packed. We had started with nothing and now had a booming business. All that hard work paid off.

A strong work ethic is an attitude and a belief, not a skill. If you have it, it is very difficult to teach it to you. Work ethic is learned, but it's learned the way all attitudes are learned—through constant exposure over a long period of time. Kids who grow up in an environment of discipline, learning from hard-working parents and role models, are more likely to learn to be hard workers themselves. When things come too easy to people, they don't understand how hard work plays into success.

Hope is Not a Strategy

I was no different from any other kid. I saw things I wanted, and I asked for things from my parents, just as we all do. One of my Dad's "Dad-isms" (which is kind of like an aphorism, except that my dad's name was Rich, not "Aphor") was, "the people in Hell want ice water." This was Dad's way of saying it's fine to want things, but just because you want it or ask for it or hope for it doesn't mean you are going to get it.

As a college football player I was, realistically, a little better than average. I was not the biggest offensive lineman, in fact, I was a bit undersized at 215 pounds. I wasn't really fast or the strongest on the team. The one thing I did have was a desire to play. I was so into playing football and getting better at my role, and of course, I was hoping to be a star. I realized right off during camp that I was going to have to work hard to get any playing time. I needed to get noticed and figured that, while starting a fight with the hard-core middle linebacker (he even had a hard-core name, Clyde Folsom) might help me stand out and get the coaches to recognize me, that strategy was also probably going to land me in the emergency room.

So I took another tack. I decided to hit full-out all the time. Every time. I would be the first one on the field, the last one off, and spend even more time in the gym after practice. I lived in the gym and worked as hard as I ever have to get better. Each day I would volunteer to be the first to go in the "bull in the ring" drill. For those who have experienced this, you get it. For those who have no idea, let me explain.

The bull in the ring is a drill where players (in my case all linemen, offense and defense) circle up with one in the middle. The object is for a player in the circle to run two to three yards and block/smash into the player in the middle. The player in the middle is tasked with blocking the oncoming player. It begins with the coach blowing a whistle, which gets feet moving, running in place. Now, the guy in the middle starts spinning around in a circle because *anyone* from the outside circle could be called to smash into him.

So here we all are, running in place, hyped up by the coaches, yelling, sweat running into our eyes and drool off our mouthpieces, just ready to smash into someone. As each is pumping his feet up and down, the coach will call out a number of a player on the outside circle (the player's jersey number usually). This is the signal for the player to run, get up a head of stem, and try to flatten the player in the middle. Of course, the player in the middle never knew where his opponent would come from (and the sadistic coaches almost always called out a number behind you). The player had to continue to move in a spinning motion in order to get ready to fend off the oncoming freight train. You get the idea, right?

Well, I decided that I was *always* going to be the first one in the ring, every time. I knew that if I worked hard, stepped up, and took the lead, I just might get noticed and get a chance to play. And I *also* knew that being first, I was fresh and it would be easier for me to fend off the guys in the outer circle!

My hard work paid off in spades. A few games into the season, I got my shot. I was tapped to start at right tackle for our big game against Penn State. (Yes, *that* Penn State.) We were playing them in State College, Pennsylvania. I had my chance to start and show them just what hard work was all about. It was the hardest game I ever played. I was up against a defensive tackle who was six feet, seven inches, 275 pounds, and I swear he hadn't been fed in a week. He was hungry for some raw quarterback, who just happened to be my roommate. Imagine if a brick wall was growling at you. Well, I'm proud to say, we won that game ten to six and the ride back was glorious!

There's nothing wrong with hope. There's nothing wrong with buying a lottery ticket once in awhile, if that kind of thing is fun for you. There's a whole section of this book coming up in a few pages about how sometimes it's just pure luck. The problem comes in when you start depending on hope and luck and lottery tickets instead of doing the work.

When you wait for something great to happen to you, you leave your fate in someone else's hands. Think for a minute about the successful people you know. How many of them got there totally by accident, without lifting a finger? Right. So don't be the person in hell begging for ice water. Be clear about what you want, know what action you need to take to get it, roll up your sleeves, and get to work!

ROLL 'EM! Roll Up Your Sleeves!

If I were the kind of guy who makes bets, I'd bet a case of signed copies of this book (and a case of beer besides) that there's something in your life right now that is—to put it bluntly—pissing you off. It's something you've been meaning to do for at least a week, and more likely for a year or more. Every time you think about it, it eats at you, but after that wave of aggravation passes, you move on to other things. Now, I don't know what that thing is for you. It's different for everybody. But I haven't met too many people in my life who don't have one.

So here's what I want you to do: Pull out a piece of paper, and up at the top, write the thing that needs doing. It could be as major as renovating your kitchen or as simple as calling your sister to apologize for the rude thing you said to her and she hasn't spoken to you since. Write it down.

Next, write a description of what "done" looks like. This can be as short or as long as you want, with as much or as little detail as you want to write, but the one thing you must include is how *you* are going to feel when you check that bad boy off your list. Write as much about that as you can. Will you be happy? Relieved? Proud? All of the above? Who will you show off your completed project to? How will your life be better for having done it? What will become possible for you? Close your eyes for a minute and imagine you are there. What is that like?

The last step of this exercise can go one of two ways. If the process you just finished did not leave you feeling like Rocky on the steps of the Philadelphia Art Museum, do yourself a favor and forget about it. This undone thing might be pissing you off, but having it done apparently won't help much, so save yourself the trouble! Pick a different dream to pursue and throw that one out the window.

On the other hand, and if you've been thinking about this thing for as long as I'm betting you have, and the idea of having it done makes you want to shout Hallelujah from a mountaintop, then the last step is the first step. Use the GPS process to set a goal around it, and make sure the first step toward getting it done is on your calendar, if not for today, at least for before the end of this week. This stuff doesn't do itself, you know. If you really want this done, you're going to have to do it. So define the steps in the process, roll up your sleeves, and get to work!

So much has been written about life balance. Why? Because balance is the difference between qualified success and total success. See, you can be a rock star in your career (figuratively or even literally), but if you are miserable in your personal life—whether it's a bad relationship, loneliness, depression, sickness, or addiction—you aren't really successful, are you? Or if you "have it all," with a nice house and a beautiful family and a car in the garage and a chicken in the pot, but you are deep in debt or desperately wishing you could do different work or feeling spiritually empty, you are not there yet.

Life balance is so many things. Sometimes it seems like the parts of your life where you need balance are polar opposites, and you have to mess one thing up to make the other thing work. So how do you get the balance you need?

First you must define it. What is life balance to you? I use a "balance wheel" to lay it all out. I define three general life growth categories—self, relationships, and financial—that I split up into nine life areas (check out the list below). Balance can mean different things to different people. It is individual, unique to you, so the first step to finding the right balance for your life is to define what that means for you.

Let's take a closer look at these nine life areas:

Self-growth
- Physical/Health
- Personal growth
- Recreation

Connection
- Family
- Social
- Spiritual

Financial growth
- Career
- Money management
- Giving back

These are the nine core areas of our lives. If you go back and look at your role map, you'll likely see that anything you have on your role map could fit into one of these nine areas. And just like with your role map, some of these may be more important to you than others. Your emphasis and priorities also tend to change over time. A single college graduate launching a new career is going to have different priorities from a soccer mom, a company vice president, or a retiree with young grandchildren. And one person could have all four of those at different times in his or her life.

Balance doesn't mean spending exactly one-ninth of your time and efforts on each of these areas. It means spending appropriate time and effort in each area according to your purpose, values, and goals. When your life is in balance, you'll know it by a feeling that time-management guru David Allen calls "being at peace with what you are *not* doing." If you are constantly worrying about work when you're at home, worrying about home when you're at work, and worrying about insomnia when you're staring at the ceiling at 2:00 AM, you are out of balance. You'll know you are in balance when you can show up completely to whatever you are doing right now, and be all in.

Balance has to start with you as an individual. Self-growth is the first step. A good friend of mine and a fellow coach and speaker, Chris Sopa, likes to say, "You cannot give what you do not have." In order to be able to live your purpose and serve your family and society the way you are meant to do, you have to be *mens sana in corpore sano*—a sound mind in a sound body. If you don't feel great, if you are tired all the time or have a bad attitude about life, how are you supposed to do any good for anyone else?

Once you have your Self in balance, it's time to make sure your connections are in balance. Your family and friends need your love and attention, as does your spiritual life, whatever that means to you. Again, this might be a big time commitment for you or it might not, depending on where you are in your life. I have two teenage daughters who need me to be there for them, and I need and want to do that. So I make sure I make time for that. If you are part of a couple, married or otherwise, that relationship needs some time and effort. Maybe you have kids or grandkids, aging parents, sisters, or brothers or cousins you need or want to be with. Maybe right now you don't have a lot of family commitments, but you have a church group, a civic organization you are in, or maybe you just have some buddies you love to hang out with. That doesn't put itself on your calendar—you have to make time.

Last but not least, your financial life needs your attention. If you're like most people, you work at least some of the time, so that has to be figured in when you are looking at balance. You also need some time to review your financial situation regularly, so you know what's going on with your bank balance, your investments, retirement savings, budgets, and so on. When you have a good handle on your finances, you know what you can comfortably spend on fun things like birthday presents and vacations, and donations you give to your favorite church or charity. This all figures into the life balance equation.

The area of financial growth (which includes career) is listed last for a specific reason. It should be the last area you work on. Work will be there when you finish working on those other areas. If you focus, as so many do, on your career, job, business, and money while forgetting about your health or your friends or family, you may find your health, friends, and family are not there when you finally get to them. On top of that, you will feel stress from these other areas that could have a negative impact on your career. So when you set out to put things in balance, start with your most important area *other than career.*

Everything changes all the time, so you have to be ready to change with it. The more you understand where you're at, the more you can be all in with what is most important to you, and the better you can serve others without using yourself up.

The Waffle

Something you're going to understand about me by the end of this book is that breakfast is important to me. I'll admit, I'm not quite as committed as that pig in the old farmer's story, but I am definitely serious about breakfast, and I am committed to serving others. Turns out these two things are related. Let me tell you a story about making waffles.

There are times when you just have to be okay with making waffles. Now, before you say, "That's it. Coach Rick has lost his mind," and throw this book in the trash, let me explain what that means. It means that sometimes you have to give back to others. Imagine you are at the all-you-can-eat breakfast buffet, standing at the waffle maker, and instead of just making your waffle and sitting down, ask yourself who else might want a waffle. Look around and you'll probably see three other hungry people waiting for you to get done so they can make their own waffles. You have two choices: You could pull your waffle out, put it on your plate and go eat, or, you could give your waffle to the person standing behind you and make another. You could even say to yourself, "How can I serve here? How can I show my servant's heart?" And if your heart is in it, you can choose to do something fun and unexpected and make waffles for everyone in line. Make a good time of it and make someone else's day. Serve someone who didn't expect to be served, and see how it plays out across the entire dining room.

Believe it or not, that's not my only waffle story.

At my house we love slumber parties. With two teenage girls we have a bunch of them, as you might expect. My greatest joy comes in the morning of the party when I get to get up early, have my coffee, and start making breakfast for the crew that has slept over.

I crank out bacon, sausage, eggs, and sweet rolls and, of course, *waffles*! I even have one of those big, round, commercial Belgian waffle makers that makes those great fluffy treats you can serve with strawberries and whipped cream on top. That is the real deal right there, my friends.

What a joy to see those sleepy faces light up when they see food and especially *waffles*! Kids love waffles (who are we kidding—*everybody* loves waffles). For me, the real joy is in making them. I get such a feeling of happiness and joy from making waffles and serving them. And it's not because I'm some kind of repressed wannabe short order cook; it is about giving back to others. You might be asking, why waffles? Why would waffles be so important to make? I could have made pancakes, used the same basic batter, which would be just as tasty but less work. But waffles, well waffles are really special pancakes. They have the nooks and crannies for the butter, special crevices for the syrup and, well, they float on the plate. And of course, they look so cool! Waffles say you care to make that little bit extra effort to go over and above to serve the people you lead; to bring a smile to the faces of the people you surround yourself with. That is the key to balance.

You'd be surprised how much you find you have when you start giving it away. Try this—when you feel your life, body, mind, time, and so on is out of balance, give something to someone who doesn't expect it. Put out that little extra effort and make it special for someone else. Give from your heart and you will see just how you find joy, peace, and balance come from right there. This is simple to understand but hard to do.

ROLL 'EM! Make time for some waffles

In the appendix of this book, you will find a section called "Balance Wheel." Flip to that page and complete the exercise, then come back here. No, really. Right now. I'm waiting . . .

Of the nine life areas, which one has the least amount of shading? In other words, where did you think you were least living up to your potential? Take a minute right now to decide what you want to do about it. Choose one goal, and write that goal on a GPS worksheet. If you have time, go ahead and complete the GPS, placing at least the first action item into your calendar for this week. If you're not quite ready to do the entire GPS, make an appointment with yourself to get it done. (May I suggest filling it out over waffles this weekend? Watch out for the syrup.)

Wouldn't life be grand if we were in total control of everything all the time? Actually, it probably wouldn't, because you'd never have any surprises. It's a moot point, though, because we don't. For everything in your life that you can control, there are ten things you can't. You can discover your life

> "Sometimes you're the windshield; sometimes you're the bug."
>
> —Mark Knopfler

purpose and do everything in your power to live it every day. You can set goals and achieve them. You can make an unwavering commitment to what matters to you, and you can work hard to build a life of balance, joy, and service. But you can't predict every single thing that's going to happen.

You can't completely eliminate all risk. Stuff happens. Fires and floods destroy homes and neighborhoods. Storms can wipe out entire towns. People get sick—sometimes with illnesses of the body such as cancer or heart disease or with illnesses of the mind such as depression or psychosis. Sometimes people hurt themselves or hurt others. This is just how the world is, and bad things can happen to you. Sometimes it's just pure luck.

It works both ways, too. Some people live one hundred years and the worst health problem they ever face is a paper cut. People win lotteries and find soul mates. Sometimes the weather is perfect on the day of the family picnic or outdoor wedding when you really need perfect weather. You couldn't have predicted or forced it to turn out that way—it's just luck.

But is luck really just pure luck, or are there things you can do to put the odds a little bit more in your favor? How do you create luck? This question is *huge* for people who are looking to create high levels of success in their lives.

How do you create luck? Can you? I believe you can. You can create luck, but you have to be there to receive it. You can win the lottery, but only if you buy a ticket. Put yourself out there. Show up completely. Look for the opportunities that may be presented. Luck will not walk into your door or house. You have to go and get it. Make luck happen.

I have had my fair share of luck in my journey through life. One of my most exciting pieces of luck was when I was able to meet the elite Navy skydiving team "Leap Frogs" at an event in our town. This led to my getting a chance to live one of my life-long dreams: jumping out of an airplane (and living to tell about it). Yes, part of this was luck. But it could easily have passed me by if I had not been paying attention. Here is how I got the luck to come to me.

Friday nights are high school football nights, and usually I love to go watch the game. But on one particular Friday I had just come off a very tough week, one that almost crushed me personally and professionally. I was not in the mood to go anywhere. Also, my friend whom I normally watch the games with was not going to be there that night. But when I thought about it, I said to myself, "Hey—I love watching the game and cheering on our local team, so I'm going to suck it up and go. I'm going to have a good time. I always do." I could have sat home licking my wounds from the week, but instead I chose to put on a positive attitude, get out, and have fun. Well, it was a good thing I did. Because on that night the powers that be had arranged to have the LeapFrogs do a pre-game show, skydiving down onto the football field.

Just getting to watch this show was great—a nice stroke of luck to put a positive spin on a tough week. But it gets better. From there I ran into another friend from my men's Bible study who was a school board member. He saw I was by myself and invited me to sit with him in the press box. Well, getting bumped to "first class" is always good, but little did I know *how* good. While watching the game and enjoying the food in the press box suite, the LeapFrog team came in to get something to eat and meet the school board members, mayor, and other VIPs. I am loving this—the luck is coming thick and fast.

Then the team leader, JC Ledbetter, has his plate of food and sees the empty chair next to me. He politely asks if he can sit there, and sits down. We get to talking, sharing stories, and finding things we have in common. We hit it off right away. During the course of the conversation I mentioned how I had always wanted to jump but I knew that I was just a little too big to do a tandem jump. (I'm a pretty big guy, you see—six foot four and weigh about 245 pounds). Tandem jumps have weight restrictions, and I'm outside the limit. Well, JC says, "No problem. You ever want to

jump and you are in Southern California, here is my card. Give me a call and I will personally take you." OMG, right? If I was one of my teenage daughters, I'd either be screaming or passing out from excitement.

The only catch is that I live in Texas. I don't really get to

Southern California very often. I wanted this so bad I could taste it, but I could not for the life of me figure how to make it happen. But you know I wouldn't even be telling this story if it didn't have a happy ending, so here is where the last stroke of

luck comes in. One of my closest friends from childhood just happens to live in Oceanside, California. A former Marine, he chose to stay put in California after he got out. A couple of weeks after the football game, he called and told me he wanted me to come out for his annual Christmas party, and he and I would host it together. The last piece of the puzzle falls into place. I was going to be in Southern California in a month. One thing led to another, I made the call to JC, and he set up a jump for three of us—my friend, his daughter, and me.

I was able to live a lifelong dream because I made my own luck by showing up and paying attention. Sometimes it just pure luck!

ROLL 'EM! Set yourself up for luck

Fortune favors the prepared mind. Think about some of the things you really want to do but it seems totally out of reach—your wildest dreams, if you will. Pick out the one you want most. Someone famous you wish you could meet? Trip to an exotic destination? Buying a fancy car or a dream house? What's your biggest, craziest wish?

Now it's time for an experiment. Put that crazy wish down on a GPS worksheet as though it was a goal. Don't worry if it's not a "SMARTWAY" to experience goal loss right now, just write it down. Now take it through the GOSAT process, focusing especially on the obstacles and their solutions. What's really standing between you and making this wish come true? You may just find that it's not as far out of your reach as you think. And when you write down obstacles and solutions—even if the solution is something as unlikely as "meet the leader of the LeapFrogs at a football game"—just the act of putting your intentions out there can create some unexpected luck in your life. It's all about paying attention, showing up, and letting those strange coincidences work to your advantage.

"Don't give up. Don't ever give up."

Many people have said these immortal words, but they came to *me* from Coach Jimmy V. It was such an honor to work with him, and frankly, I didn't even realize how great it was when it was happening. I learned from him how to get knocked down and get back up. I'm a big guy, as I said before—bigger than most. I also filled out relatively early in life. In fact, it has been said, looking back on old pictures, that I was the only one who had been eating hamburger. I had the body of a grown man at sixteen. Because of this I was always seen as older, which allowed me to be a camp counselor and to play with the college kids at times. I will say I somewhat kinda, sorta, held my own most of the time. This helped me form the belief that I can always be better. I could not be satisfied with just okay. I was playing up with the big guys and I had to step my game up a notch in order to stay there.

I enjoyed watching my teammates from school watch me play, take the lumps dished out by the college players, and at least hold my own. I wasn't the smoothest, but I hung in there and always tried to get better and to learn something and try it next game. What a life experience!

I took away two lessons from it: 1) never give up, and 2) play the game a little bit out of your league sometimes. Sure, it can get pretty rough when you get out there with the big boys. But it's the only way you're ever going to know what you are capable of. Nobody ever got into the big leagues without taking a risk. Getting out of your comfort zone helps you figure out where your comfort zone ought to be.

I have learned that when you play a little out of your league, you become just that much better. You are forced to step up to the level of competition you are facing. I did it when I had to play against older, better players at summer basketball camp. You can do it by paying attention to what the successful people in your life are doing; get involved with what they are doing. Try something new that will take you outside of your own comfortable paradigms. When you step into a new arena with "bigger and stronger" players, your game will naturally improve. It may take awhile, but hang in there and keep pushing forward.

Coach Valvano was not born a championship-winning basketball coach. I was not born a successful executive coach and speaker. We both had to stretch our limits and then go beyond them to find out what we could do, and so do you. What can you do? How are you ever going to know if you don't get out there and give it a shot?

Marianne Williamson said, "Your playing small does not serve the world." Shoot—your playing small doesn't even serve you, much less anybody else. So don't play small!

I said I was going to accuse you of greatness at the end of this book, and I'm doing it now. You are *great,* and you can tell everybody Coach Rick said so. You have everything you need to be successful and happy, and to serve the world in your own unique way. Nobody else can do what you are here to do.

By this point in this book, if you have read the words and more importantly taken the *actions,* you have a pretty good idea what your purpose is, and what you want to do with your life. So there's nothing left now but to do it.

There are some tools in the back of the book that may help you. You've already been back there to check out the balance wheel and the GPS. There's also "Coach Rick's 12 Commandments for Success" that will sum things up and provide a quick review in a few weeks or months when you need a refresher but don't necessarily want to read the entire book from cover to cover again. Use the tools. Write in the margins, make copies of the GPS worksheet, and write in your journal every day. Set goals, achieve them, and set new ones. Get help from mentors, teachers, and coaches. Find ways to stay inspired every day. That's what I do, and that's what all successful people do.

Get your attitude right. Focus on the basics. Commit to do what has to be done. Take action.

Roll up your sleeves and get to work!

I'd like to thank all the people who helped to make this book possible.

First, huge thanks to my friend, colleague, and writing collaborator Tracy Lunquist for all her help, words, and support in making this book a reality. Her way of making my words clear and allowing my voice to come through is uncanny. She saw something in me and challenged me to make it a reality. So we did.

Thanks to my lifelong friends and brothers who lived these stories with me and have inspired me to be a better man. Diamond Dallas Page, Steven Moreira, and Mike Bolen are role models and heroes to me.

Thanks to my mastermind group and co-authors of *Selling for Geniuses* for showing me that writing can be fun and fulfilling, and that I can make a difference by just being me.

Thanks to my NSA friends who *always* cheered me on and pushed me when I was struggling to take the next step or write the next page.

Thanks to the host of other characters (and I do mean *characters*) who are a huge part of this book and its content.

Thanks to my family: My sister, Denise, brother Michael, and my daughters, Megan and Lauren. Your love and encouragement means everything to me. I was able to write this book because of your belief in me and the inspiration you have provided for me. I love you all forever.

Finally, I thank my Lord and Savior, Jesus Christ, for loving me unconditionally and letting me share these life lessons with you.

Coach Rick Kolster is a Certified Business Coach, founder, CCO of Peak Performance Development, and the CEO of the Peak Performance Group. Rick's ability to speak the *bald truth* about personal and professional success has made him a sought-after speaker, facilitator, and coach to organizations and their top-level executives across the United States and Canada.

Coach Rick's expertise in sales, leadership development, and team performance, along with his straightforward, no-holds-barred style make his presentations, books, and blog articles as easy to understand as they are valuable. Rick is a co-author of the 2009 book, *Masterminds Unleashed: Selling for Geniuses,* as well as the popular blog, "The Bald Truth."

Coach Rick has more than thirty years of business experience in numerous industries ranging from hospitality to industrial sales and manufacturing to television programming. He and his team help individuals and organizations to recognize unhealthy paradigms, change attitudes, and meet the challenges of the modern business landscape.

But let's cut to the chase here. What you really want to know is: is Coach Rick a real person I can call on to help me achieve my goals and those of my company? And the answer is *yes*! Here's the *bald truth* about how to get in touch with Rick:

Rick Kolster

Peak Performance Group
300 State St., Suite 92891
Southlake, TX 76092
817-748-RICK (748-7425)
www.CoachRickKolster.com
Rick@CoachRickKolster.com

Coach Rick's 12 Commandments for Success

1. **Do It Now**! Procrastination is the largest nation in the world, and it's high time you renounced your citizenship. There is no better time than the present to get something done. Sure, there will be times when it is inconvenient or impossible to take action on something you know you need to do. Okay, I get that. But then you have to ask yourself: if not now, *when?*

2. **If not now, *when?*** This is not just some empty motivational cheerleading motto. This is a real question. When? As in, what week of your calendar are you going to pull up *right now* and write in an appointment with yourself to get moving on your goal, Without a deadline, a goal is nothing but a nice idea.

3. **Take initiative, get creative, be innovative.** See, this is how you know Coach Rick gives you value—this is three commandments in one! Whatever plans you are making, whatever ideas or problems are running around in your head, they are there so you can do something with them. So get started. Put your hand up and commit to doing what needs to be done. Find solutions to the problems. Get around the obstacles. The guy who starts on pole position doesn't always win the race, but he sure has an advantage over everybody in his rear view mirror.

4. **Give back more than you take.** Do all this because it will make you happy, yes. But do it too because God did not put you here just to take up space. You are here for a reason, and the ways that you give and serve are meant to make the world a better place. Be a servant. Be generous. Leave this world better than you found it.

5. **Make a decision, right or wrong, but make something happen.** I'm not saying you should never think things through, but don't let yourself get stuck in "analysis paralysis." Look at your situation, look at your priorities, and make a choice. If you are right, great! If you are wrong, you won't make that mistake again. Either way, you are in motion. Getting yourself pointed in the right direction is just details.

6. **Ask questions if you don't know.** Nobody knows everything. It's not a crime to ask a question! The crime is when you're drowning under something you don't understand or can't fix and you don't ask for help. Most people are wired to help each other. If you need help, don't just pretend you are invincible and have all the answers. Ask.

7. **If it's broke, fix it. If you can't fix it, find out who can.** Whether it's a busted coffee maker or a messed-up marriage, too many people stuff their broken things into a closet (literally or figuratively), and hope some magic will happen to make it better.

81

If a miracle is going to happen, it's going to be because you made it happen. Face your challenges head-on, fix what you can fix yourself, and call in backup if you need it.

8. **Positive attitude + Belief in yourself = Success.** Even if you flunked math you can figure this one out, right? Notice this doesn't say "be born rich, get a PhD, be connected to famous people, be tall and handsome." That's all great and everything, but you don't need any of it. What you need is a positive attitude and a belief in yourself. When you believe in your own worth and value, you will figure out how to make money, do well at school or work, and be confident when you meet people. Never let anybody tell you that someone else is better than you. God gave you everything you need.

9. **Negative attitude + Doubt in yourself =** *Failure.* People say things to themselves that they would never say to another human being. Don't tolerate that kind of smack talk in your house. Doubt will eat you alive if you let it. Don't let it.

10. **Think before you speak!** Rotary Club International's "Four-Way Test" is a pretty great way to check yourself before you open your mouth. Ask yourself if what you're about to say is true. (Seems like a no-brainer, yet how many times have you lied or been lied to?) Ask yourself if saying it is going to be fair and beneficial to everyone around you. And ask yourself if it will build better relationships. If it doesn't pass muster, ask yourself what you ought to say instead—or even better yet, just listen.

11. **See the job as something you do, not as something you gotta do.** Remember the Seven Dwarfs from the *Snow White* movie? "Whistle while you work," they would sing. Even Grumpy was a hard worker, and it was because they had purpose in their work that they could go to it every day with focus and discipline. You can pass on the whistling if you want, but adopt the attitude that your work is a service and an honor. Find the joy in it, and notice how much faster and better it gets done.

12. **Be Nice!** You can be aggressive in the pursuit of your goals without being a jerk. You don't have to climb over anybody else to get to the top of your ladder, and you don't have to push other people down to build yourself up. Rise up and lift others with you. Be a role model of kindness at the same time you are a role model of achievement and success, and people will follow you anywhere.

Follow and use these rules, and you will expand your horizons, both professionally and personally.

Example:

The Balance Wheel is a tool you can use to take stock of how things are going in your life. To use it, you'll need a pencil or something else you can use for shading (a crayon works great if you have one).

Consider each of the nine areas on the outside ring of the wheel. Imagine that the curved line closest to the center of each section is zero, and the outside edge is 100 percent of your full potential in that area of your life. So if you shaded in the entire career section, for example, it would mean that you were completely satisfied with your career—you've totally lived up to your full career potential. Shade in each section starting from the center and moving toward the edge to represent what percentage of your full potential you feel you have satisfied in each area.

Once you have done all three of the sections of a fundamental section (for example, spiritual, family, and social are the parts of the fundamental section "relationships"), you can evaluate your relationship potential overall. Same drill, same person—shade it in from the center toward the edge to show the percentage of your potential you feel you have satisfied.

Notice that this wheel is not about how much money you make, or how many hours a day you spend with your kids or how many books you read last month. It's up to you to decide how *YOU* define "full potential" and how you do your percentages. You could be a single guy with no plans for marriage or kids, and if that makes you happy, your "family" section may be at 99 percent. Don't let someone else's definitions of happiness or success determine how you do your balance wheel.

Once you're done, take a look at your wheel. Where are you doing great? Where could things use some work? If you filled any section in less than 50 percent, there's work to do there. Most likely you don't feel too great about how things are going in that part of your life, and you'll need to roll up your sleeves and get to work on that. In other sections, you filled in at 80 percent or more, you're probably pretty happy. Good for you! Just remember what it took to get you there, and make sure you don't get lazy or complacent in those areas.

Now, let's look at the wheel overall. If you took away the black lines so all you saw was the shaded parts, how would your wheel roll? Would it be nice and smooth, or would it be like driving down a road full of potholes? If some areas are a lot different than others, you're out of balance. What would you do differently to smooth out the ride?

What about the fundamentals? This wheel looks somewhat like it has a tire on it, right? The nine areas on the "tire" affect the ride. But the three parts of the "wheel" hold the tire in place. If there are big gaps there, it may be tough for you to keep rolling at all. What needs work? What goals and actions are needed? Who can help you? How soon can you get that help?

Once you've had some time to think through where you are and what you want to do about it, set up some SMARTWAY goals using the GPS Worksheet. Decide what you need to do, roll up your sleeves, and get to work!

On the next page is the GPS worksheet, as explained in section 2.6 of the book. For a free, downloadable, full-size copy of this worksheet, please visit www.CoachRickKolster.com.

Peak Performance **GPS**

GOAL ID: _____   DATE: _____

GOAL	POSITIVES	NEGATIVES

TARGET DATE: _____

OBSTACLES	SOLUTIONS	ACTIONS		TIME	WHO
a		a1 _____ a2 _____ a3 _____ a4 _____ a5			
b		b1 _____ b2 _____ b3 _____ b4 _____ b5			
c		c1 _____ c2 _____ c3 _____ c4 _____ c5			
d		d1 _____ d2 _____ d3 _____ d4 _____ d5			

www.mypotentialplus.com   Peak Performance Group GPS

86

This is the three-column Beliefs Worksheet, as explained in section 1.2 of the book. For a free, downloadable, full-size copy of this worksheet, please visit www.CoachRickKolster.com.

My old beliefs	How they have NOT served me	How they have NOT served others

1. Do It Now!
2. If not now, *When?*
3. Take initiative, get creative, be innovative.
4. Give back more than you take.
5. Make a decision, right or wrong, but make something happen.
6. Ask questions if you don't know.
7. If it's broke, fix it. If you can't fix it, find out who can.
8. Positive attitude + belief in yourself = *Success*
9. Negative attitude + doubt in yourself = *Failure*
10. Think before you speak.
11. See the job as something you do, not something you gotta do.
12. Be Nice!